THE HANDMADE SKATEBOARD

DESIGN & BUILD a CUSTOM LONGBOARD, CRUISER, or STREET DECK from SCRATCH

MATT BERGER

—Founder of SK8Makers

SPRING HOUSE PRESS

Publisher: Paul McGahren

Editor: Matthew Teague

Designer: Carol Singer

Layout: Benjamin Rumble

Illustrator: Matt Berger

Photographer: Matt Berger, except where noted

Cover photo: Jonathan Binzen

Copyeditor: Deborah Golden

Indexer: Holly Day

Spring House Press

3613 Brush Hill Court

Nashville, TN 37216

ISBN: 978-1-940611-06-8

Library of Congress Control Number: 2014943104

Printed in the United States of America

First Printing: September 2014

To learn more about Spring House Press books, or to find a retailer near you, email info@springhousepress.com or visit us at www.springhousepress.com.

This book is dedicated to my two smart, strong, and creative daughters.

The world is your workshop,
and knowledge and curiosity are your sharpest tools.
You can build anything.

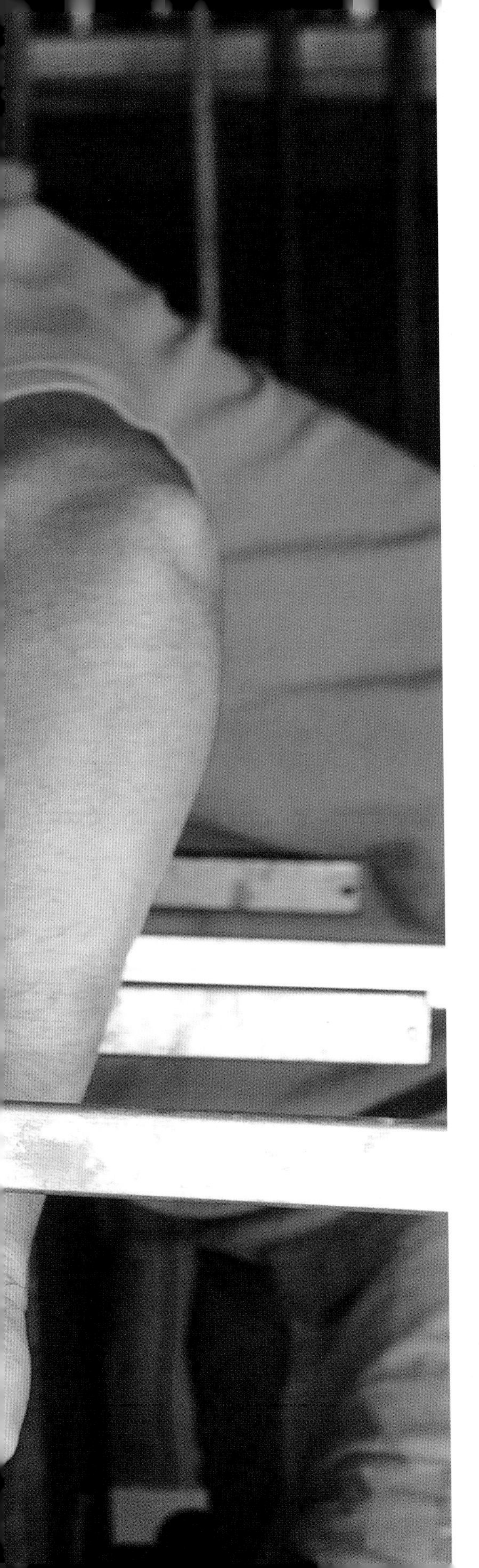

CONTENTS

See the Sunny Scenic
WORLDS GREATEST ELECTRIC RAIL SYSTEM
Miles of Relaxing Trolley Lines
2700

CHAPTER 1

INTRODUCTION
HISTORY OF THE SKATEMAKER

The true story of the skateboard is not unlike those heard around Silicon Valley in the early days of personal computing and the Internet. Some guy tinkering in his garage comes up with a smart idea that works, catches on, and maybe even changes the world.

You could be talking about Hewlett-Packard or Powell-Peralta, the creation story is pretty much the same.

For the skateboard, it started with a simple idea: a plank of wood, with two sets of wheels, that you stood on and pushed to go. Then through decades of innovation and entrepreneurial zeal, the idea gave rise to a billion-dollar industry and cultural phenomenon, influencing music, movies, fashion, and pop culture. These days it's mostly the riders who get the credit. But the skateboard maker played a big part in transforming that plank of wood with wheels into a device capable of launching riders into amazing aerial acrobatics or reaching downhill speeds of epic proportions.

A GARAGE-SHOP INVENTION
The skateboard is an American innovation born in the garage. Modern-day garage shop makers keep the craft alive.

The modern-day skateboard has come a long way since the earliest garage-shop creations by Southern California's scrappy young surfers. These early pioneers collectively invented the pastime more than a half-century ago when they ripped the metal wheels from their strap-on roller skates and nailed them to a plank to see how fast they could go. Those primitive handmade decks of the 1950s may have started it all, but they were really just a means to an end. Bored surfers looking for a thrill when the waves were flat made do with hacked-together decks that offered the next best thing: the experience of catching a wave on concrete.

As popularity of skateboarding grew beyond the shores and valleys of Southern California to Brooklyn, Chicago, and around the world, so did the expectations of daredevil riders. The DIY-deck culture that started it all—hacking together boards from found and borrowed parts in the garage—couldn't keep up with the demand. And why should it? An entire industry of specialized makers was champing at the bit to innovate.

IN THE BEGINNING
A Roller Derby skate deck was a commercial response to the fast-growing DIY movement.

EARLY INNOVATIONS IN THE GARAGE SHOP

In the annals of skateboard-making history, commercial makers went through a period of discovery and rapid innovation in the 1960s and early 1970s to push the skateboard into the mainstream.

As more and more kids hit the pavement with their DIY decks, manufacturers saw the opportunity to build products that met their needs. It started with toy companies cashing in on the craze with gimmicky products like The Scoot Kit and the Roller Derby skateboard with metal wheels, which more resembled a toddler toy than a modern high-performance skateboard. These were commercial responses to the hacked decks kids were building in their garages using scrap wood and roller skate wheels. It was a sign of the times.

Before long, a run of skater-led companies took root with specialized products designed to actually meet the needs of riders. One of the first was a pioneering surf shop in Dana Point, Calif., launched by a woodworker/surfer named Hobart Alter, whose nickname—Hobie—has since become an internationally known brand in the skate, surf, and sailing action-sports industries.

A decade after Hobie had turned his hobby—making handcrafted balsa wood surfboards—into a lucrative beachfront business, he used his woodworking skills to take skateboarding mainstream with the Hobie Super Surfer Skateboard. The solid wood deck was composed of multiple hardwoods glued together into a striped flat deck, much like the vintage pinstripe deck project in chapter 4. Dozens of other startup skatemakers followed suit with similar products with names like the Sidewalk Surfer and the Hang Five.

About 30 miles away, just north of Hollywood, a dad and his sons were about to give the skate industry an even bigger boost when they opened an inland surf shop in Valley Village, Calif., called Val Surf. The landlocked shop quickly saw an opportunity to bring the beach culture to the valley. They struck a deal with the Chicago Roller Skate Company to produce the first trucks specially designed for skateboarding, improving on the metal and clay roller skate trucks and wheels that riders had been using to date.

In 1964 the Hobie Skateboard Team was assembled to demonstrate the trickery one could achieve on new

HUMBLE BEGINNINGS
Before urethane and even composite clay, the earliest iterations of the skateboard featured metal wheels salvaged from old pairs of of roller skates.

VINTAGE CRUISER
Inspired by the hardwood skateboard decks of the 1950s, this retro deck is fun to ride when decked out with modern trucks and wheels. Learn how to build your own in Chapter 4.

decks like the Hobie Super Surfer. The team showed off its tricks nationwide when it was invited to give a skateboarding demonstration on national television. Soon, skateboarding was showing up in magazines, television, and in the movies; John Lennon was even photographed on one.

By 1969, many more Southern California surfers had turned into skatemakers, taking their DIY designs to the commercial market. These boards were designed to accommodate specific uses like downhill speed riding, freestyle, or street skating. With his Makaha skateboard company, a Southern California lifeguard and entrepreneur named Larry Stevenson moved the industry beyond flat when he invented the kicktail—an innovation that is probably the most important functional design in skatemaker history. A few years later, Stevenson won a patent for his design.

The next decade moved skatemakers farther out of the garage and into the mainstream. In 1972, an enterprising young surfer named Frank Nasworthy introduced the urethane wheel to skateboards, kicking the stakes up a notch.

Two years later, in '74, a skateboard entrepreneur named Richard Novak introduced precision ball bearings to the mix; by year's end, he'd sell more than a million of his Road Rider Wheels.

This was also the era of Dogtown and Z-Boys, and the edgy skateboard counter-culture was spreading far and fast. Designing and manufacturing skateboards was becoming a highly profitable business. By the end of the decade, a top skater like Stacey Peralta could bring in six figures to design a new skateboard deck for a manufacturer and lend his name to the logo and packaging.

CONCRETE WAVE
30 miles inland in Valley Village, Calif., the Southern California surf shop Val Surf was hard at work inventing the modern skateboarding industry.

A SHORT HISTORY OF THE SKATEBOARD

Before you design and build your first skateboard deck—or even your fiftieth—it's a good idea to take a look back at the last half-century of skateboard design to see what's been done, and how makers and riders arrived at the most popular modern deck designs.

There's no better way to experience that history than taking a trip to the Skateboard Hall of Fame in Simi Valley, Calif., where skateshop proprietor and deck collector Todd Huber has amassed an amazing collection of more than 5,000 skateboards and memorabilia from every era since the beginning: endless stacks of no-name DIY decks from the 1950s and '60s. And at least one deck of every iconic brand—and usually more than one—from the 1970s, '80s, '90s and 21st century.

Huber welcomes tens of thousands of visitors each year to his indoor skatepark, skateshop, and museum, where decks of all shapes and sizes cover every inch of wall space.

IN HIS ELEMENT
A walk thought Todd Huber's Skateboard Hall of Fame is a history lesson on all things skateboard.

COURTESY ACTIVE RIDE SHOP

THROUGH THE AGES
Vintage skateboard decks from the 1960s and '70s blanket the walls at Skatelabs Indoor Skatepark in Simi Valley, Calif., home to the official Skateboard Hall of Fame, where Todd Huber has amassed a gigantic collection of decks representing milestones in skateboarding history.

A SHORT HISTORY OF THIS SKATEMAKER

My path to building a perfect skateboard deck is a microcosm of the history of the American skatemaker. Like the first deck hackers of the 1950s, my early introduction to building a skateboard came in the form of a simple wood plank with recycled wheels.

I wasn't a skateboarder at the time. I was an enterprising undergrad in a college beach town and I liked to make things from wood. I had access to a student craft center filled with top-of-the-line tools and equipment for ceramics, bike repair, photography, and woodworking. Creative young people who believed they could make anything frequented the craft center. The crowd and the whole vibe of the place inspired me to tackle projects I would have never pulled off otherwise.

I picked up a part-time job in the woodshop sweeping sawdust, tuning the tablesaw and bandsaw, and teaching basic woodshop safety classes to the coeds. Many students were there to build wooden models for engineering or architecture classes. Others were eager freshmen looking to meet people or learn something new. During fraternity rush season every year, classes filled up with pledges on assignment to make an oak paddle engraved with their prospective house letters. Not long after the finish dried, their shiny new paddles were used against them in a great wallop.

But every now and then some lanky kid in a backwards hat would come in with a sheet of plywood

THE 1940s & '50s: THE BIRTH OF THE DIY DECK

Some time during the 1940s and 1950s youth across the world—from Southern California to Paris—collectively invented the skateboard by hacking together a plank of wood and reclaimed roller-skate wheels in their garages and basements, and then hit the pavement.

File photos from Getty Images dating back to as early as 1944 capture gangs of kids clamoring for the next ride on primitive wood contraptions decked out with wheels. These were distant ancestors of the modern skate deck, but the seeds were planted.

It was the Southern California surfer community that can take

EARLY SPECIMEN
Trucks and wheels on the earliest skateboard decks were ripped from roller skates and screwed to a plank of wood.

THE CALIFORNIA LIFESTYLE
A classic woody makes its way through Newport Beach, California, near the epicenter of skateboard history.

asking to borrow a jigsaw and a power drill. I watched as he roughed out clunky surfboard shapes from cheap plywood, drilled crooked truck holes, and then rode off victoriously on his hacked-together longboard deck. The deck was crude, but just good enough to cruise from class to class and impress the ladies with his easy-going attitude and baggy board shorts.

I was impressed, but I also knew enough about woodworking to know that there was a better way.

I quickly realized that if I could apply my woodworking skills to build better quality skateboard decks in popular shapes and designs, there was an endless supply of college kids willing to part with weekend beer funds to buy one.

The trouble was, I didn't ride a skateboard. In the third grade, when all my friends rode Powell-Peraltas, my parents cheaped out and bought me a toy-skateboard that could barely roll downhill. Since then, my only run-in with the skating was through endless nights of *Skate or Die* on my Nintendo 64 video game console.

I had no idea what made a skateboard good or how one was constructed. So I did what any good inventor does and reverse engineered the best decks I could find. Then I developed my own building methods.

most of the credit for taking the skateboard out of the garage and back alleys and into the mainstream. Surfers embraced "sidewalk surfing" as a hobby, lifestyle, and adventure sport, turning to it when the waves were flat. It was the era of the Endless Summer, and the skateboard served as a perfect companion for the beach-bum counterculture crowd.

The concept of a rolling plank of wood was revolutionary enough that there was little innovation in skateboard design and construction during its adolescent years. The trucks and wheels were borrowed from roller skates—no one had yet designed a set specifically for a skateboard. And the deck shape remained mostly square, small, and flat.

The first commercial deck came out around 1959. The Roller Derby (see photo, page 4) mostly emulated the DIY-deck designs that inspired it. Others that followed were more toy than sporting good.

It didn't take long to get hooked on making longboards and riding them around town. I hacked my way through the first batch and sold the lot to friends and curious onlookers. Then I used the proceeds to fund new batches that improved upon my process. I tried out different materials and adhesives to get just the right amount of flex and strength. I engineered my own shop-made clamping press to improve the glue-up process and accommodate more interesting designs and bends. I tried out new shapes and sizes based on feedback from customers.

Obsessed, I started churning out batches of longboards between classes, each one signed, numbered, and stamped with my self-proclaimed brand: Bergerboards.

By the time I graduated from college I had pressed my fiftieth deck. My crowning achievement: a 39-in long curly maple longboard cruiser with a black and white checkered pinstripe running down the center. I dubbed it the "checkerboard." A few years later, it got stolen from my apartment in San Francisco; I hope the jerk at least used it to bomb Lombard Street.

A BOOMING BUSINESS
Modern skateshops are now standard fare all over the world. This Venice, Calif., shop sells everything from laid back longboards to complete street skate decks.

THE 1960s: THE GOLDEN AGE OF SKATEBOARDS

Skateboarding came into its own in the 1960s, moving from a niche, neighborhood adventure-sport to a national sensation. The skateboard showed up in magazines, movies, music, and television—everyone from Gidget to Lucille Ball was seen riding one.

As its popularity grew, so did the business of making and selling skateboards. In 1963, the owner of an inland Southern California surf shop called Val Surf teamed up with the Chicago Wheels company to modify the company's trademark roller-skate wheels into something better suited for the skateboard. New skate companies emerged, like Hobie and Makaha, as skateboarding's popularity grew.

SIDEWALK SURFING
The early 1960s brought a wave of skate makers producing flat plank decks like the Skate 'n Glide, Sokol, and Roller Derby.

THE SKATEBOARD SHOP GROWS UP

A few years after the stolen checkerboard incident I found myself back in the woodshop with a new urge to make skateboard decks. My new job as an editor at a woodworking magazine gave me access to a 5,000-square-foot woodshop filled with the best power tools known to man and a brain trust of woodworking experts who took breaks from building beautiful furniture to help me apply a craftsman's skills to making skateboard decks.

Looking over their shoulders, and practicing what I saw on lunch breaks and after work, I earned the equivalent to a master's degree in woodworking. I know why wood shrinks and expands with changes in humidity. And I learned how to anticipate that movement in a particular piece of wood so that the things I build accommodate changing conditions without cracking or warping or twisting. I learned the physics of plywood and how to bend wood and make it hold its shape. And I was introduced to the vast world of specialized woodworking tools and equipment designed for the home shop that could empower even the most inexperienced weekend warrior to cut and finish wood into a quality piece of furniture. I reveled in learning a new craft, even if I was the only guy cruising on a longboard through my Connecticut neighborhood.

Then one day I stumbled upon a husband and wife team from Toronto, Canada. Ted Hunter and Norah Jackson were marketing a simple, self-contained kit that included everything an ambitious kid needed to build a professional skateboard deck from scratch on his kitchen table. Like me, Ted and Norah weren't skateboarders when they started dabbling in the business of making skateboards.

The brainchild of Ted and Norah, the Roarockit skateboard kit, builds on a simple woodworking concept called vacuum pressing. With vacuum pressing, thin layers of wood are glued and stacked on top of a molded form, placed inside a plastic bag where the air is evacuated using a vacuum pump, forcing the veneers to form around the mold. Once the glue cures, you're left with a bombproof finished deck in a shape that matches the molded form.

What is special about the Roarockit method of making a skateboard deck is that it doesn't require an expensive vacuum pump system, yet it yields the same result as a high-quality factory-made deck.

In 1965, skateboarding made the cover of LIFE magazine. That same year, a shaggy-haired John Lennon was photographed on one, flashing peace signs and everything.

Like anything fun and cool, a backlash was inevitable. Skateboarding was not a crime in 1966, but parents and the media started to treat it like one, condemning the sport as unsafe for kids and urging city bans on the sport. Its popularity plunged.

But a core group of SoCal enthusiasts who started it all stuck around and pushed the skateboard to new limits. In 1969, it paid off for surfer and skateboard entrepreneur Larry Stevenson when he invented the kicktail, altering skateboard design forever. He won a patent for his innovation two years later, describing the kicktail as "conveniently positioned for a person to depress with one foot in order to facilitate spinning the skateboard through a wheelie maneuver or the like."

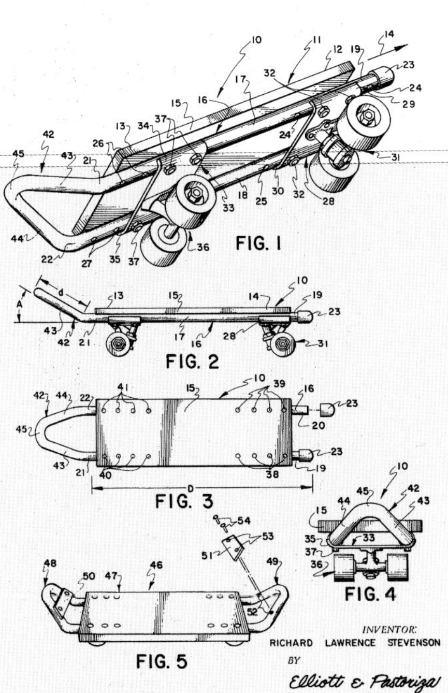

LET THERE BE KICKTAIL
The original patent diagram for the "Skateboard with inclined foot-depressible lever" a.k.a., kicktail.

DECK IN A BOX
The Roarockit DIY skateboard kit includes all of the tools and materials to press a seven-layer maple skateboard deck.

PRESSED FOR CHANGE

To date, the skate industry has relied religiously on ginormous two-part hydraulic presses to laminate the seven layers of veneer into a molded skate deck. It would cost you at least a few thousand bucks to set up a similar operation in your garage. The Roarockit kit, meanwhile, relies on a thick plastic bag, a foam mold, and a simple hand pump, just like the one you can pick up at any local wine shop to pump the air out of a half-filled wine bottle before storing.

Thanks to Roarockit, rather than putting all my creative energy into inventing a laborious process and the jigs and fixtures to make even the simplest skateboard decks, I was freed up to focus my innovative efforts on the actual deck—its shape and design, the materials, the complex curves and graphics.

Ted and Norah quickly realized they were onto something with their kit. So they patented it: US Patent No 7,132,030 and CA Patent No 2,390,264 describe the Roarockit method of "manufacturing a skateboard deck from a plurality of thin layers of veneer capable of conforming to a contoured surface under pressure, comprising the steps of. . . ." Essentially, it's what I described a few paragraphs back.

More than a dozen decks into my time with the Roarockit kit, I came across the most important Craigslist find in my life: an electric-powered vacuum pump and vacuum press table like the ones I had learned to use a few years earlier in the office woodshop. These tools automated the hand-pump process that made the Roarockit kit a chore.

The listing was from a cabinet shop in South Central Los Angeles that was going out of business after 30 years. Its owner/proprietor—Joseph Sicolo—had just turned 90 and was ready to hang up his tool belt, including his lineup of industrial-grade vacuum veneering equipment. Sicolo had made his living creating fantastical, curvy interiors for L.A.'s wealthiest residents—million dollar jobs designing for Hollywood's lavish excess. In the 1980s, Sicolo claims, he was the first to install a television set into the foot of a bed that raised and lowered by remote control.

When I arrived for a look at the equipment I was not disappointed, except for the fact that I didn't have a bigger truck. That day I took home a 10 cubic foot per minute (cfm) VacuPress pump with an automatic on/off switch that keeps pressure at a consistent rate for as long as needed.

Since the late 1980s, woodworkers and cabinet makers have used vacuum press systems to build

1970s: THE INDUSTRIAL AGE OF SKATEBOARDS

The *eureka!* moment for the skateboard came in the early 1970s when an enterprising, young surfer named Frank Nasworthy introduced the world to urethane wheels, replacing the metal and clay wheels of the past. His Cadillac Wheels were made of a rubbery plastic that were more forgiving when rolling over sticks and rocks and cracks, and gave the rider much better traction to grip the road at high speeds and tackle more gnarly terrain.

Eureka struck a few years later when skateboard entrepreneur Richard Novak came up with a revolutionary new ball bearing system called the Road Rider wheel, which improved the ride even more. Novak

curved furniture and architectural components of all sizes and shapes—and, in many cases, to laminate inexpensive materials with exotic veneers. The method was born out of the aircraft manufacturing industry dating back to World War II, says Darryl Keil, whose company VacuPress (yes, the same one) was the first vacuum pump on the market designed for woodworkers and furniture makers.

"That's how they built the Spruce Goose," Keil says, referring to the famous aircraft from Howard Hughes.

Keil has literally written the book on the subject: *Vacuum Pressing Made Simple*. He explained the simple concept behind vacuum veneering: It starts by sucking the air out of the vacuum bag. "You can do this with a vacuum pump, a hand-powered pump, or even with your own lungs," Keil explains (though he didn't recommend the latter).

Anything placed inside the bag is compressed under high atmospheric pressure as if a heavy weight were pressing down on top of it. The VacuPress system, for example, is designed to keep a bag somewhere between 13 lbs. and 14.7 lbs. of atmospheric pressure per inch. That means that a stack of veneer measuring 8 in. wide by 30 in. long—roughly the size of a skateboard deck—has the equivalent of 3,120 lbs. pressing down on top of it (8 in. x 30 in. = 240 square in. x 13 lbs. per square inch = 3,120 lbs.) There's also another element at work called "defusing" which adds to the compression.

Armed with my new equipment, I spent the next few years in my garage, vacuum pressing decks for friends and family, pushing the limits on design and construction. And having a lot of fun.

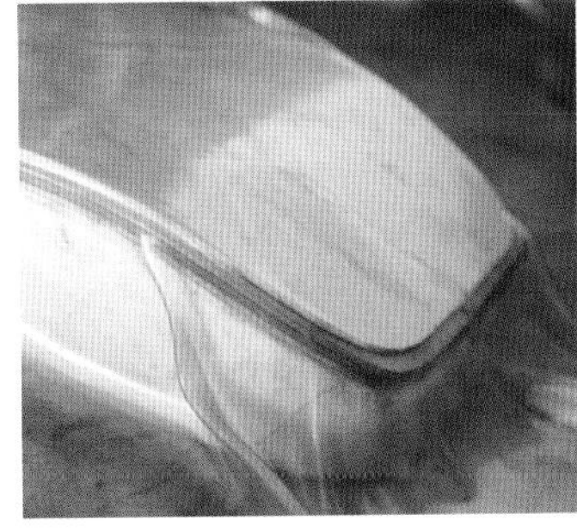

THE WOODWORKER'S SOLUTION

Used by woodworkers far and wide, a vacuum pump and press is designed to glue up multiple layers of veneer against a shaped form to create a molded piece of plywood, or a skateboard deck.

did well, selling more than a million of his enclosed bearing wheel sets by 1975.

Eureka hit a third time when Ronald Bennett introduced a new style skateboard truck with a big red rubber bushing where the kingpin attached to the T-shaped hanger. It gave the rider control to adjust the tension and make the deck harder or easier to turn.

These innovations and more brought a major revival of the sport. While the Venice Beach Dogtown skate scene was taking shape west of L.A., new skateboard brands emerged. Skateparks opened across the U.S. welcoming a new generation of skaters, and the start of billion dollar business was underway.

Until, toward the end of the decade, the tide turned against skateboarding once again.

DOGTOWN

A well-ridden Alva skateboard, circa 1977, the namesake brand of Venice Beach skateboarding pioneer Tony Alva. Designed for shredding empty SoCal swimming pools.

MANUFACTURING REVOLUTIONIZES THE SKATE DECK

This same rapid innovation in tooling and technology moved forward not just me, but the entire skateboard industry. By the 1980s, deck manufacturers were employing advanced machinery on a gigantic scale to produce hundreds of thousands of decks a year.

Tim Piumarta is the head of research and development at the mega skateboard company NHS, Inc., the company founded by the bearings baron Robert Novak. He's also responsible for mega brands like Santa Cruz Skateboards and Independent Truck Company.

In a phone call from his Santa Cruz, Calif., research and development shop, Piumarta retold the story of how he helped set up the company's first skateboard factories in the early 1980s in northern Wisconsin, home to what he still considers the best hard maple on earth for making skate decks.

"Santa Cruz had its factories in the forest," Piumarta said. "I didn't believe in shipping all that maple to California, so we put our skateboard factories in a couple of places in northern Wisconsin that made fine cabinetry; they needed the extra revenue. We set up three shops there, and one in Santa Cruz, and produced about 900 decks a day."

It was the heyday of the American industrial age, when manufacturing jobs helped prop up local economies in small towns across the U.S. And it was good business. "Ninety percent of the workforce was moms re-entering the workforce," Piumarta said. "I used to tell the kids: 'Your skateboards were made by moms.'"

But as the cost of manufacturing products in the U.S. became prohibitive (hey, Mom wants a good paycheck, too) and free trade agreements sent manufacturing jobs abroad, Santa Cruz Skateboards and the rest of the industry sent most of its production overseas, too.

"It costs more money to knock down a tree and peel it into veneer in the U.S. than it does to ship the tree to China and have them do it there from start to finish and ship a finished deck back to Long Beach," Piumarta explains.

"We still employ people cutting trees, peeling and putting on trucks, but a whole lot of it went to China."

To make a blank skateboard deck in the U.S., it would cost as much as $75, even under the most effective business conditions. The going rate for a blank deck from China? About $15 or less.

THE 1980s: THE RISE OF THE UNDERGROUND

In the early 1980s skateboarding had again fallen out of the popular spotlight. Still, pockets of skateboard subculture dug in and pushed the sport in a new direction. The decade gave birth to the backyard skate ramp, fueled by punk rock music, a bad attitude, and the motivation to go higher and faster and do more tricks.

Meanwhile, the skateboard deck shape was also morphing radically. New manufacturing processes that pressed layers of thin veneers into decks allowed makers to create new shapes and contours. Decks were stronger and bigger, and riders could go places and do things with them that they never could before.

By the end of the decade, the first decks to feature a kick in the nose hit the market, allowing riders to do the same kind of vertical tricks on the nose that they could on the tail, only in reverse.

SKATEBOARD GETS RADICAL

Moving into the mid to late 1980s, the skateboard deck took on a radically new shape designed for thrashing ramps and curbs.

HERE COME THE '80s
An early Santa Cruz skateboard deck hangs on the wall at Skatelabs Indoor Skateboark in Simi Valley, Calif., home to the official Skateboard Hall of Fame. Santa Cruz was one of the first to develop a large-scale manufacturing process for high-quality maple decks.

ONE OF A KIND
This handmade longboard is handcrafted from maple and bubinga hardwoods, laminated with a sheet of thin plywood in between, and shaped with hand tools.

THE SK8 MAKER VS. GLOBAL INDUSTRIALIZATION

This new era of global industrialization is where my personal analogy with the history of the skateboard maker diverges. It's no longer cost-effective to run a small skateboard company in the U.S., and the handful of startups that pull it off are few and far between.

The mega manufacturers who can churn out millions of decks at low cost and record speed each year in Chinese factories employ proprietary equipment and techniques that you and I can barely imagine. Drills that can cut all eight truck holes in a stack of skateboard decks in a single pull. CNC machinery to create CAD-perfect molds used by giant two-sided hydraulic presses that can press dozens of boards in a few hours. Computer-operated cutting bits that can stamp out a deck to within 1⁄64 in. of its specified shape. And industrial grade machines that apply multicolored heat-transfer graphics in minutes.

In a way, this factory automation has propelled skateboarding to become a multinational, multi-billion dollar industry. The best skateboarders require this level of precision in each deck. Otherwise, they could end up on their tails after a failed trick. Or much worse.

As the commercial deck relies more and more on a process that is out of reach for mere mortals, there is great value in the handmade and one of a kind. Making things from scratch is a dying art on the brink of extinction. It was pushed to the edge when public schools dismissed woodworking classes and turned the school woodshop into a computer lab. And when you separate society from how things are made—even a skateboard—you lose touch with the labor and the materials and processes that contributed to its existence in the first place. It's not long before you take for granted the value of an object. The result is a world where cheap labor produces cheap goods consumed by careless customers who don't even value the things they own.

It doesn't have to be that way. And you can start with the skateboard. That's my vision for SK8Makers; to create a global community of DIY board builders who together fuel a cottage industry of handmade skateboard decks.

Give a kid a skateboard, she rides for a month. Teach a kid to build a skateboard, she rides for a lifetime.

THE 1990s: GENERATION X GAMES

In 1995, the first X Games took skateboarding into the mainstream once again, mesmerizing kids around the world with aerial acrobatics mastered on backyard ramps and city streets and sidewalks.

To meet the growing worldwide demand, deck manufacturing headed overseas, where skateboards could be produced faster and cheaper. The industry started its consolidation into a few mega deck manufacturers and the skateboard design also unified around a common popsicle shape. To this day, the symmetrical design remains an industry standard.

Meanwhile, a maker community was heading back into the garage to hack the skateboard. It was the dawn of the Internet and access to materials to build skateboards were available to anyone with a dial-up modem. In 1994, a group of skaters in La Jolla, Calif., hacked together a longboard deck from an old snowboard, giving birth to Sector 9 longboards.

A CASE FOR DO-IT-YOURSELF

Everything that goes into making a professional skate deck in the factory—from the preparation of raw materials, to the design and engineering of the assembly line to the construction processes and precision factory automation—is unmatched by man and shop tools alone. And industrial solutions are only getting more refined as technology advances and hardcore riders push skateboard companies to new limits.

At best, the sweetest deck you could ever make in your garage shop today might just match the quality and reliability of the best commercial decks available at your local skateshop. And it may even cost you more to make your own. The specialty maple veneer and equipment necessary to build a high-quality skateboard deck aren't cheap.

So if it isn't cheaper, or faster, or even always better to go the DIY route, then why should you make your own longboard or skateboard deck from scratch?

2000s: SKATEBOARDING EVOLVES

By the turn of the 21st century the symmetrical popsicle deck was pretty much the standard. While the shape stayed the same, the materials and manufacturing processes improved. New adhesives were making decks stronger and lighter, with more "pop." Computer operated machinery was improving the manufacturing process and lowering costs. And some board makers were experimenting with new materials like carbon fiber, Kevlar, and fiberglass.

Meanwhile, skateboard hackers were pushing the boundaries once again, outfitting decks with off-road monster trucks and wheels. A small group of SoCal longboarders took a cue from ocean paddle-boarders and started propelling themselves up and down trails with flexible poles. Longboarders in Northern California harnessed wind-power, using kites to pull them around.

ROAROCKIT METHODS PUT INTO PRACTICE
This street deck was constructed from seven layers of maple veneer using a simple foam form and a hand-powered vacuum bag.

A PASSION FOR MAKING THINGS FROM SCRATCH

When you make your own skateboard you have the opportunity to create something that is perfectly tailored to you: a deck that matches your height, your weight, your center of gravity, your skill level, and your intended use.

More importantly, making your own skate deck allows you to design the perfect deck to fit your personal style; to make a statement about who you are and what you do. I'm not saying there's anything wrong with off-the-shelf and mass-produced. In fact, many people prefer it that way. But sometimes you want to stand out. To be different. One of a kind. That's exactly what you get with a handmade skateboard deck.

A revolution in inexpensive, easy-to-access tools and materials is also making it possible to create anything from scratch with near-professional quality at home, even if you're building them one at a time. Access to equipment and low-cost suppliers has long been a luxury monopolized by big manufacturers. Now these things are just a Google search away.

The 3D printer is probably the best example of where the revolution in DIY manufacturing is headed. In the old days, an inventor needed $100,000 in tools, equipment, and space before he could ever produce his first $2 widget. Today, with a $2,000 desktop 3D printer, some cheap plastic filament, and CAD software downloaded for free off the Internet, an inventor can print out his first 20 widgets—each one slightly improved over the previous—on his kitchen table.

The same is true for skateboards. Once closely guarded by the industry, the raw materials and tools used to make a professional deck are readily available on the Internet, and even at your local hardware store or lumber yard.

These days, anyone with the desire and a little motivation can become a skatemaker.

Put simply, the idea that you can create something from nothing is empowering. You get a certain satisfaction from building something practical and functional using raw materials and starting from scratch that you simply can't replicate by buying it off a shelf. Making your own custom skate deck fulfills a primal urge that goes back to the cave days when man and woman figured out how to rub two sticks together to make fire.

This passion for making things has inspired me to build all sorts of things I never would have expected. This passion is what got me into woodworking. Now I can drop a tree in the woods, cut it to size, shape it, and join it with other pieces of wood to make beautiful objects that my great-grandkids will enjoy some day. There are worse ways to spend your time.

I learned to use a MIG welder on a whim and six months into it was commissioned to build a custom canopy bed. Every time you acquire a new skill, you open yourself up to new opportunities. One of them just might stick.

2010s AND BEYOND: SKATING INTO THE FUTURE

The street deck still reigns, but the second decade of the 21st century shows promise for new innovations for the skateboard. Advances in battery and small motor technology have made possible the long-imagined dream of a practical motorized skateboard. A handful of hackers have developed gas and electric-powered boards that can travel 15 mph for as far as 20 miles.

The ZBoard (pictured right) was one of the first to catch on. Pressure-sensitive buttons on the front and back of the deck propel the deck forward or back on any terrain or incline. The ZBoard attracted hundreds of thousands of dollars on the crowd-funding site Kickstarter. Soon after, a group of Silicon Valley dropouts followed suit with the electric Boosted Board, earning a half-million dollars from crowd funders. Now when is someone going to invent the hoverboard skateboard?

A MAKER'S GENES
Here I'm experimenting with furniture making using a MIG welder at my former, tiny shop in San Francisco—located in an industrial complex made out of converted metal storage containers.

My mom owned a yarn shop for 25 years selling wool and patterns for knitting and crocheting. She taught my brothers and me to knit hats and socks as soon as we could hold the knitting needles without poking each other in the eye. Though I never would have admitted it to my junior high friends at the time, I appreciated learning this handy skill. Just think, if I were stranded on a desert island, I could knit myself a stylish wardrobe with just a few sticks and handmade twine spun from palm fronds.

HANDMADE FURNITURE
I designed and built this "Horseshoe Armchair" from mahogany with ebony accents. Similar to a skateboard deck, the curved parts are constructed by laminating thin layers of wood against a mold.

REAL SK8MAKERS KNIT SOCKS
My maker habit started early. As the son of a yarn store owner, I learned to knit and sew before I could ride a skateboard.

CHAPTER 2

the COMPLETE ILLUSTRATED GUIDE to SKATEBOARD DESIGN

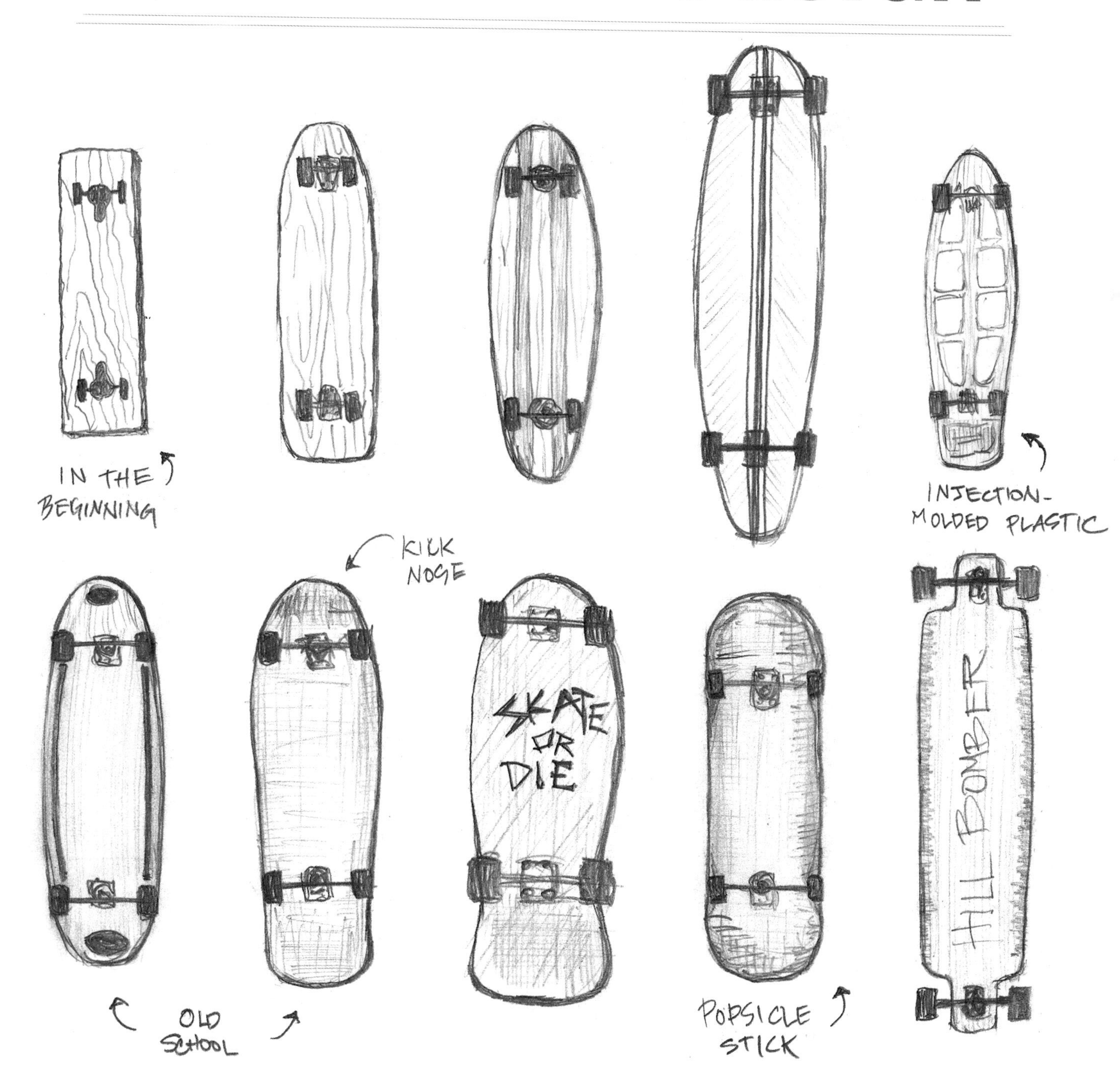

A good skateboard is like a good pair of shoes. It should fit comfortably, and the best ones are designed specifically for their intended use. In the same way hiking boots are designed for traversing dirt and rocky trails, or basketball shoes are designed for vertical leaps and agile turns, different styles of skateboard decks are designed to accommodate the demands of different riding conditions—speeding down a hill, dropping in on a half-pipe, or cruising down the boardwalk.

The skateboard may have started out as a flat plank, but it didn't stay that way for long. Makers have radically re-imagined the skate deck by inventing and refining new design elements that deliver specific function from form. Adding shape to the board increased the strength and function of the deck. The evolution to concave bends and kicktails increased the strength of the deck and made it more versatile.

But it's not just function that inspires skateboard design. Fashion and pop culture have played an important role in design. Through the decades, the skateboard deck has gotten wider and then narrower, longer and shorter, and taller and lower to the ground. Sometimes for good reason, sometimes not. And, as fashions do, about every decade they come back around again.

THE EVOLUTION OF SKATE DESIGN
Since the beginning, the size, shape, and design of the skateboard deck has ebbed and flowed with the changing trends. Borrow from these examples when designing your own skateboard.

the goods

TOOLS
Pencil, eraser, ruler or straightedge, tape measure, right-angle square, scissors, compass, protractor, round objects of various diameters for drawing curves.

MATERIALS
Roll of 24-in.-wide white paper.

EQUIPMENT
Drawing table or flat work surface with good light.

ACCESSORIES
Skateboard trucks for sizing and laying out truck holes.

THE ANATOMY OF A SKATEBOARD

KICKTAIL

The kicktail was the first major innovation in skateboard design. Just adding a simple bend to the end of a skateboard deck gave the rider controlled leverage that made possible almost every skateboard trick that came after it, from the ollie to the rail slide. The steeper the kick, the more leverage it provides, to a point.

WHEEL SPAN

Just like the distance between wheels on a car, the distance between the front and rear trucks on a skateboard deck will affect how it turns. The further the trucks are apart, the wider the turns it will make. The closer the trucks, the sharper the turn. A wide wheel span also requires a wider stance so long-legged riders might prefer a deck at the high range of the recommend wheel span.

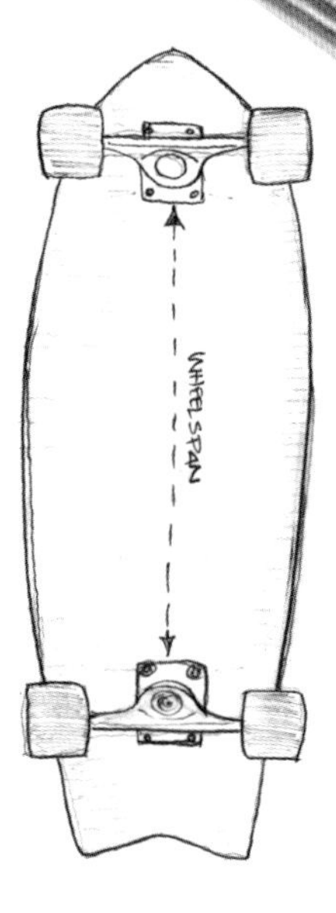

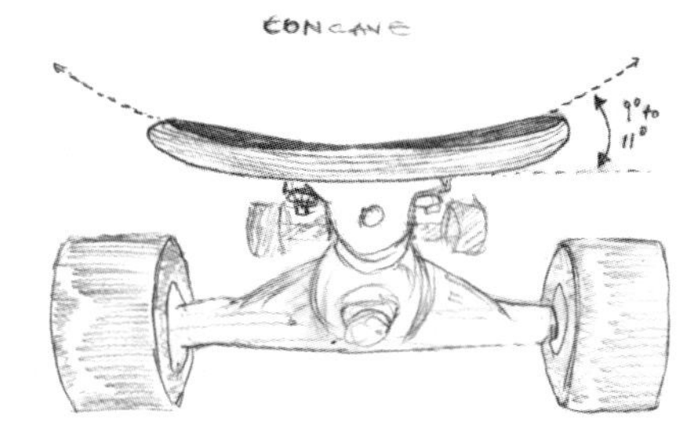

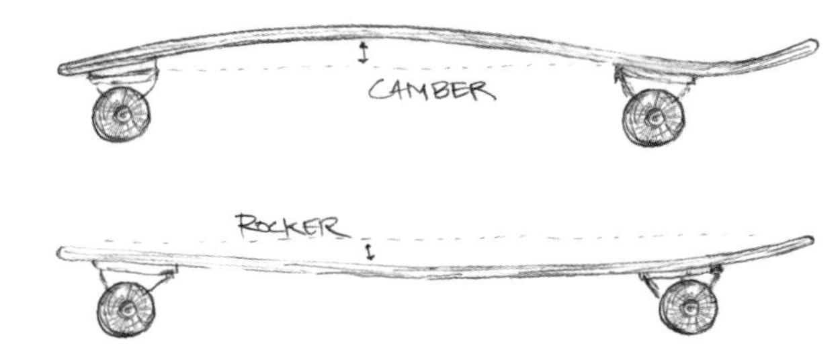

CONCAVE

Concave is the width-wise curve on a skate deck. Flat plywood is strong thanks to the cross grain direction of the alternating plies of wood that weave the fibers into a strong and durable sheet. Now add some curve to that lamination and its strength increases even more. These days, almost all skate decks incorporate some kind of concave to create a lip along each side of the deck.

CAMBER AND ROCKER

The gentle, end-to-end curve on many longboards and cruiser decks offers the rider a pleasant bounce to absorb the shock of bumps and dips during a ride. When a heavy rider stands on the deck, his weight should just about flatten out the deck. The opposite bend is called "rocker."

NOSE

For a long time, the nose of the skateboard just pointed the way for the rider. Then came the skate ramp and the "bowl," which inspired skaters to enter a trick from either direction, or switch their point of leverage sometimes in midair. A flat nose did nothing to prevent your foot from slipping right off. Around 1989 the first commercial decks hit the market incorporating a pronounced kick nose. Since then, the nose of a street deck has evolved into a near mirror image of the tail.

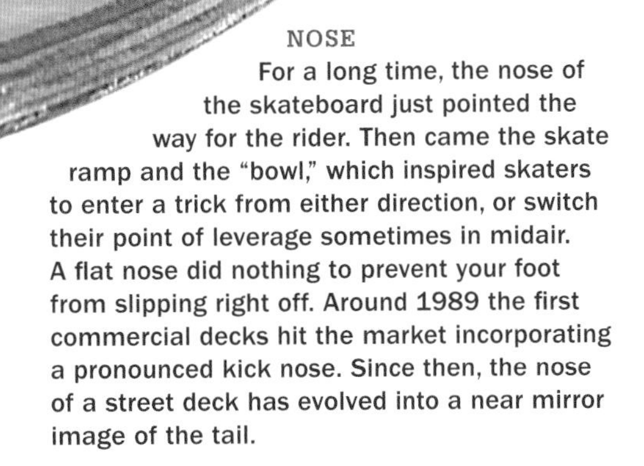

NOT ALL PLYWOOD IS CREATED EQUAL

If a skateboard is just a piece of shaped and molded plywood, then you can judge the quality of a deck based on the same principles you would use to judge the quality of a sheet of plywood at your local home center. The good stuff looks the part. It's flat and smooth and clean and the show surface—the top and side profiles—are nice to look at. It's consistent in thickness throughout—which means whoever made it did a good job gluing up the thin layers of wood veneer that comprise it. And it is measurably flat, and free of knots and voids.

Meanwhile, the cheap stuff also looks the part. Plywood—or a skateboard deck—made from poor-quality veneer plies may show knots or streaks of natural discoloration in the wood. The cheap stuff is probably a little warped or twisted. And if it's not yet, it will be soon enough. If any of the inner layers have knots or voids, those can create a weak spot in a deck that can cause it to fail if hit in the right spot with just enough force. Finally, a bad-quality glue-up can mean it is more likely to get damaged or delaminate under dramatic temperature changes or the hard use of a rider.

Hard maple, mostly grown in Canada and the northeastern parts of the U.S., is the premier hardwood species for making skateboard decks. Before they're turned into thin sheets of veneer, these dense, magnificent maple trees reach as high as 120 feet into the air, and grow as wide as 3 feet in diameter. Take a drive through New England in fall and you'll see old-timers tapping these sugar maples to collect sap to turn into delicious maple syrup for your pancakes and waffles. Not that cheap stuff that comes in a lady-shaped squeeze bottle at the grocery store. I'm talking twenty bucks a pint.

"The best hardwood managed forests in the world are in north central Wisconsin," says Tim Piumarta, research guru at NHS Inc., which distributes Santa Cruz, Indepentent Truck Company, and many others. The intensely cold weather produces the densest logs this side of Canada, he says. "The East Coast is too warm, so the density of the wood is not as good."

"Until the China log buyers came along, all the wood [for skateboard decks] came out of north central Wisconsin," he added.

QUALITY VENEER FOR A QUALITY DECK
Hard maple veneers are the go-to choice for pressed decks. These top-quality veneers are free of voids and splits, and using them guarantees a bombproof deck.

YOU GET WHAT YOU PAY FOR
Peel off the grip tape on a cheap, toy-store skateboard and you're likely to see something like this: cheap plywood with cracks, knots, and voids patched with putty. This weakens the deck, making it easy to break.

READ THE END GRAIN
The circumferential rings seen on this piece of ash lumber go in a diagonal direction. Boards with this grain orientation are know as rift-sawn.

COURTESY NINA BERGER

BACK TO THE BEACH WITH SOLID WOOD

A plank of hardwood lumber is also a fun option for building a throwback deck like the vintage pinstripe project detailed in chapter 4. However, a board constructed from a single plank of wood has limited use. It lacks the flexibility and pop of a plywood deck, which means it won't absorb bumps, dips and drop-ins and can be less comfortable to ride. A solid wood skateboard deck is also likely to be a little heavier than plywood alternatives. To achieve the same strength as plywood—enough to hold up to the weight of a rider—a solid wood deck needs to be thicker.

When it comes to making a deck from solid wood, hardwoods are preferable to softwoods. In addition to maple, other commonly available hardwoods include oak, birch, poplar, and alder. Avoid softwoods like pine, Douglas fir, and redwood. While they're lighter than hardwood, these softwoods dent and ding easily and can hold less weight.

GOING OLD SCHOOL
While veneers make up the bulk of the skate decks manufactured today, building a deck out of solid wood is easy and harks back to the heyday of early skatemakers toiling away in their garages.

PVA GLUE RULES

Skateboard makers have traditionally reached for good-old fashioned waterproof wood glue—the yellow stuff—to assemble the plies. Its official name is polyvinyl acetate, or PVA glue, and it's widely available at any hardware store, big box store, or even grocery store. You might have seen it under the brand name Elmer's. The product I prefer is Titebond III. It's the third-generation woodworking glue from Franklin (Titebond I and II are runners up in quality), and it's derived from the company's industrial-grade product PVA-SK8, which as you might have guessed by the name, was originally designed for the skateboard industry.

The holy grail in skate deck adhesive is a two-part epoxy. It's unmatched when it comes to strength, stability, water resistance, and holding a shape. But working with epoxy is a pain, especially during the high-stakes, high-pressure process of the skate deck glue-up. Also, you'd need to spend a lot of money on the off-the-shelf stuff. While some big manufacturers have figured out how to use epoxy in their manufacturing process, I don't recommend it for garage shops.

CHOOSE THE RIGHT GLUES
DIY skateboard makers don't have to look far for a good quality adhesive. Popular manufacturers sell both outdoor and water-resistant polyvinyl acetate (PVA) wood glues that are perfect for the job.

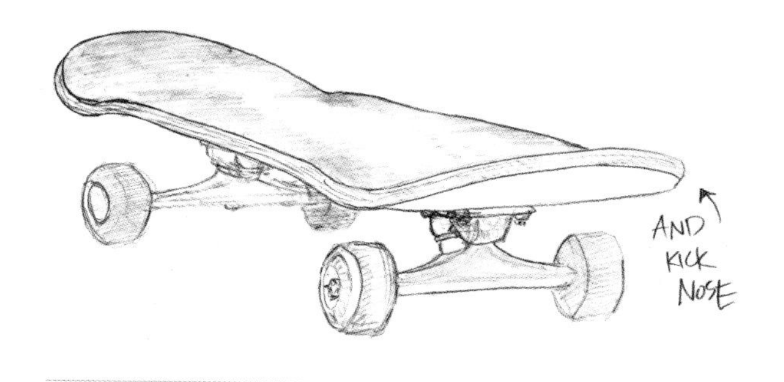

SKATE DECK

DESCRIPTION:

When most people think of the skateboard, they imagine the traditional street deck—a popsicle shaped skateboard with a kick in the tail and the nose, and a concave curve across the width that offers a good grip for your feet while adding extra strength to the deck. Professional skate decks from top manufacturers are mostly the same, differentiating themselves with graphics and small variations in size, shape, and contour. Steer clear of the cheap skate decks available at toy stores and sporting goods stores; these are typically made from subpar materials and parts.

SHAPE:

The modern street deck is mostly symmetrical from end to end with a matching rounded nose and tail. The kick in the tail and nose allow either end to serve as a leverage point during tricks. The nose is actually slightly longer than the tail on most street decks when measured from the end to the first set of truck holes. These decks are concave across the width, creating a lip along each edge. The curve is slightly more pronounced over the wheels to serve as fenders. Skate decks are generally all the same, however brands and manufacturers differentiate their products with slightly modified shapes and dimensions.

RIDER PROFILE:

Because the skate deck is the most ubiquitous style of skateboard on the market, it's used by all types of riders from professional skaters and aspiring pros to adventurous types, from students to dropouts, and adventurous tykes of any ilk. Technical riders that inflict abuse on a board can burn through a deck in about a month. However, most riders hold on to these boards much longer.

USES:

A standard skate deck is the most versatile skateboard in terms of uses. For the average rider, these decks are ideal for getting from here to there quickly. For the daredevil rider, a skate deck is ideal for getting from here to there slowly, shredding a few curbs, hand rails, and obstructions along the way. For pros, the modern skate deck is what enables them to perform mind-boggling tricks and take on half pipes, swimming pools, and whatever other obstacles get in their way.

CONSTRUCTION NOTES:

A standard skate deck is constructed from seven layers of 1⁄16 in. thick hard maple veneer laminated with PVA wood glue and pressed to a complex form. The maple layers are arraigned so that two layers have the grain running from side to side, and five layers have the grain running from end to end. This cross-grain lamination ensures that the deck stays flat and true. Most decks are decorated with heat-transferred graphics applied to the bottom side of the deck and the top surface is covered in grip tape.

RECENT INNOVATIONS:

The modern-day skate deck arrived in the 1990s. Since then the design has only changed slightly. In the last few years, big deck manufacturers have improved on the construction process and are experimenting with new materials to improve the strength and rideability. For example, some decks are laminated with epoxy adhesive instead of wood glue. And some makers have swapped out the Maple veneer layers for fiberglass and synthetic materials like carbon fiber and Kevlar.

DIMENSIONS:

From 7½ in. wide to 8½ in. wide. 29 in. to 32½ in. long.

WHEEL SIZE:

Wheels for a street deck range in size from 51 mm to 60 mm, and have a hardness ranging from 78a to 100a. For technical and street riding, the smaller and harder the better. For cruising and around-town riding, go bigger and softer.

WHEEL SPAN:

About 14 in.

TRUCK SIZE:

Depending on the deck width, the trucks should measure about 8 in. wide. Independent 129 mm trucks are the industry standard. You'll also need a thin riser to soften the connection where the trucks attach to the deck, and a set of 7⁄8-in. hardware.

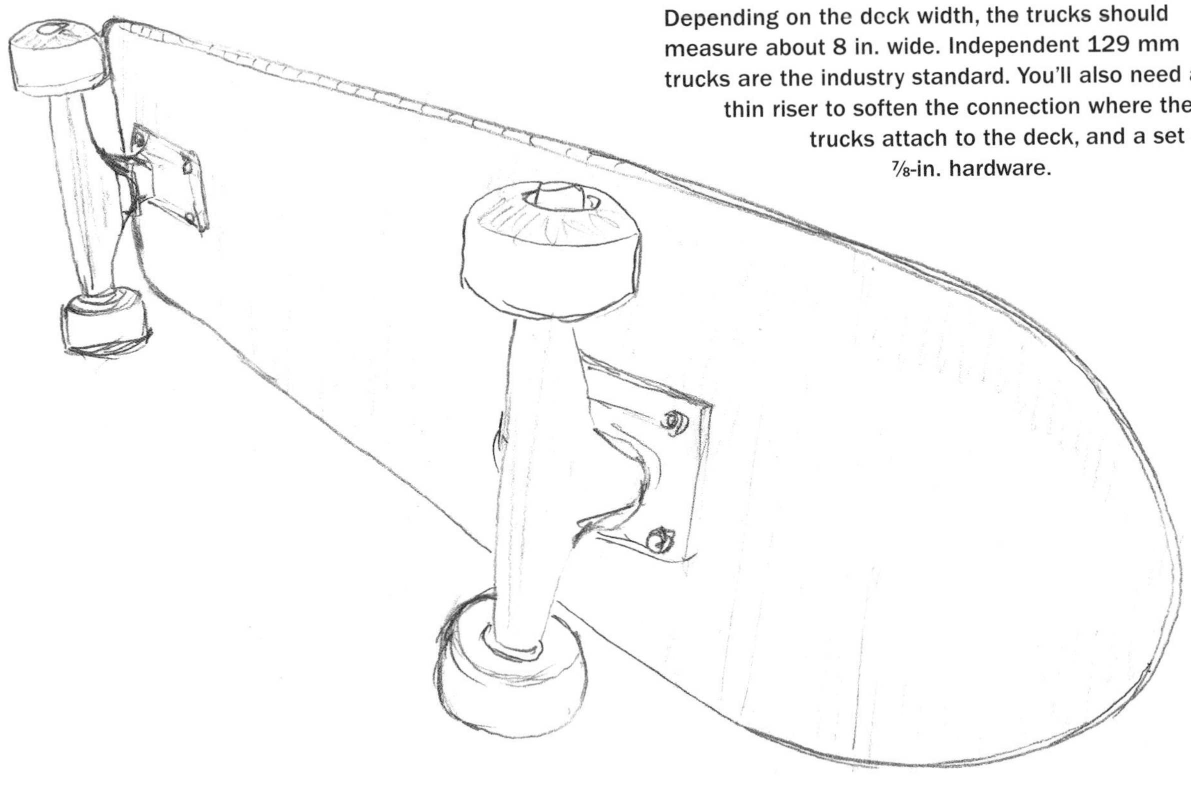

CLASSIC LONGBOARD

DESCRIPTION:

Over the past few decades, the classic longboard skateboard has given rise to a subculture in the skate world that mostly co-exists alongside the street skater community. Longboard skateboards are inspired by 1950s- and '60s-vintage wooden longboard surfboards and have a similar shape, form, and function. Like their successors, longboard skateboards are designed to provide a fun, easy, laid-back ride.

SHAPE:

Longboards come in a variety of shapes, the most common of which is the classic pintail: a surfboard shape that leads with a soft round nose, widens at the center, and then tapers into a tail. These decks often have a concave curve across the width; some have a slight upward curve from nose to tail known as camber. Kicktails are optional and few feature a kick in the nose. Longboard skateboards are longer and wider than the standard street deck and give the rider more surface to put their feet and shift their weight. They also sport bigger wheels that are set farther apart, raising the deck higher off the ground to provide a more cushioned ride. Because the trucks and wheels are big and tall, a longboard deck often has fenders that prevent the wheels from making contact with the deck when leaning into a turn. Fenders can be cutaway, carved in a cove shape, or molded with extreme concave to follow the radius of the wheel.

RIDER PROFILE:

These days you can find just about anyone riding a longboard—from small tykes to dads and moms, and every age, size, and skill level in between. Because these decks are big with a soft, cushiony ride, they're perfect for beginners and old people like me who have taken to the skateboard later in life and need more help staying balanced and upright. But that's not to say the kids don't love them, too. Neighborhoods around the U.S. have growing populations of longboarding teens and tweeners.

USES:

The ideal location to ride a longboard is a long, winding path or open road with little to no car traffic: bike paths, beachfront boardwalks, and low-traffic roads. Thanks to the big, bouncy wheels, longboard skateboards can roll right over rocks and twigs that would send a street deck rider flying through the air, so they're able to navigate more terrain. Longboards aren't light or agile, so they are less optimal for areas with lots of obstacles like curbs and stairs.

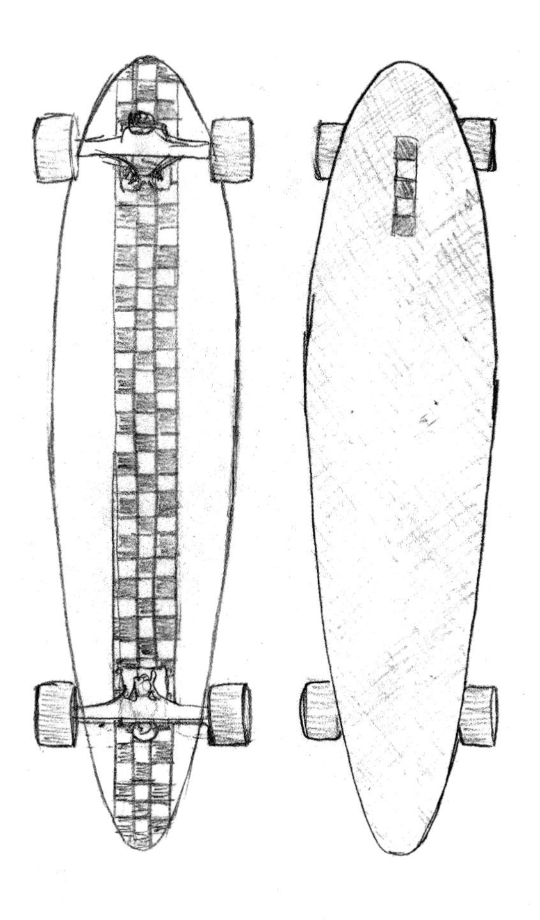

CONSTRUCTION NOTES:
Longboard skateboards are most commonly constructed from seven to nine layers of ¹⁄₁₆-in.-thick hard maple veneer laminated to a form. But they can also be made from solid wood or alternative materials like bamboo, fiberglass, and other synthetics. When laminated from seven layers of maple veneer, the veneers are laminated with wood glue so that two layers have the grain running from side to side, and five layers have the grain running from end to end. To strengthen a longboard, add two more long-grain layers of maple veneer. The graphics on longboards also come in a wider variety, from heat-transferred graphics to decorative wood veneer.

RECENT INNOVATIONS:
Since the early 1990s, when commercial longboards from Sector 9 first hit the market, a ton of innovation has occurred to improve the design and rideability. The most striking innovations are in the trucks: some feature a reverse kingpin that provides greater stability and better turning than standard street deck trucks. Southern California longboard maker Carver has gone a step further with its unique truck system designed to feel like you're riding a wave on concrete.

DIMENSIONS:
From 8¼ in. wide to 10 in. wide by 36 in. to as much as 50 in. long.

WHEEL SIZE:
Wheel sizes for longboards range in size from 60 mm to 100 mm, and typically are on the softer side with a hardness of about 78a to 90a. The general rule is the bigger and softer the wheel, the smoother and softer the ride.

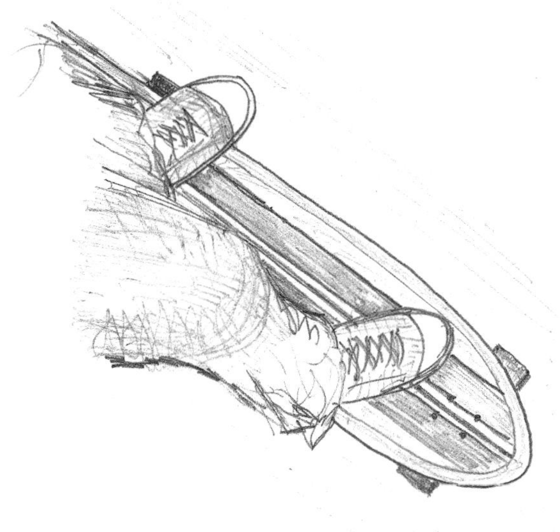

WHEEL SPAN:
The distance between the front and back trucks on a longboard vary depending on the length of the deck, from as short as 18 in. to as long as 40 in. The wider the span, the wider the turn.

TRUCK SIZE:
Depending on the deck width, longboard trucks start at about 8½ in. and go up to as wide as 10 in., or 139 mm to 210 mm. Some riders prefer the style with a reverse kingpin over standard trucks for better turning.

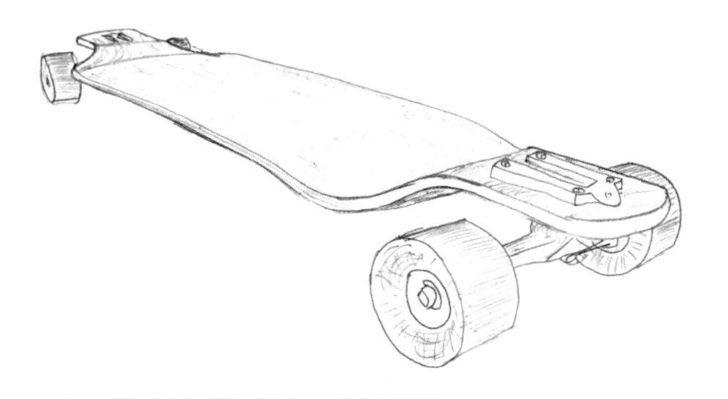

DOWNHILL LONGBOARD

DESCRIPTION:

One of the earliest niches to emerge in skateboarding was the downhill, in which riders descend steep hills at record speeds (much like with downhill snowboarding). Its roots are inland, from the Inland Empire of Southern California to the center of the U.S. where bored teenagers with lots of guts bomb steep and winding roads for the fun of it (and the adrenaline rush). Downhill riding has long been an organized sport for speed and distance contests and slalom racing.

SHAPE:

Downhill decks are specialized to help riders make it down steep hills alive—offering more stability and speed and better handling than a classic longboard. Some of the most extreme downhill riders have been known to push their deck to speeds topping 65 miles an hour. At that speed, riders require hairpin agility, extreme stability, and total control. The shape of these decks are built to accommodate: They are big and lay low to the asphalt with a wide wheelbase. They often feature cutaway fenders to provide lots of clearance for the wheels when making sharp turns. The contour on a downhill deck can range from mostly flat to slightly concave to extreme "drop-through" decks in which the center section of the deck is a few inches lower than each end of the board.

RIDER PROFILE:

Downhill longboarding requires two important components: access to long, steep well-paved roads with little traffic; and a lot of guts. Neither of those things is easy to come by, which is why downhill skateboarding remains a narrow niche. Some cities, including Los Angeles, have even outlawed the sport of "bombing hills" for safety concerns.

USES:

The primary use of a downhill board is to bomb hills at top speeds. Riders slide and carve their way down, controlling the speed with a series of sharp switchbacks, much like in skiing and snowboarding. Extreme uses also include para-skateboarding—in which the rider is pulled by a hand-held parasail—and dog-sled skateboarding, which requires an energetic and well-harnessed canine to pull you like you're in the Iditarod. Downhill decks can also be used for cruising, even though they are built to handle a much more ambitious ride.

CONSTRUCTION NOTES:
Downhill boards are more likely to be made with experimental materials like fiberglass, epoxy, and Kevlar. But essentially, they follow the same construction process as traditional skateboard and longboard decks: Layers of material are laminated against a mold. While some designs are relatively plain when it comes to shape and contour, they also are available in a "drop-through" style, which features an extreme bend and special truck mount, where the trucks fit through a hole in the deck and attach from the top. This allows the deck to lie lower to the ground.

RECENT INNOVATIONS:
Downhill deck makers are continually innovating to support faster speeds more safely. This means getting the deck to sit lower and remain stable at high speeds. While some of that innovation is changing the shape of the deck, much of it is focused on the trucks, wheels, bearings, and hardware.

DIMENSIONS:
From 8¼ in. to 10 in. wide by 36 in. to 44 in. long.

WHEEL SIZE:
Optimum wheel sizes range from 68 mm to 75 mm, with a hardness in the 78a to 88a range.

WHEEL SPAN:
Depending on the length, wheelspan ranges from 20 in. up.

TRUCK SIZE:
The best trucks for downhill skateboarding are wide and feature a reverse kingpin to grip the road and offer better stability, anywhere from 180 mm to 210 mm, or about 10 in.

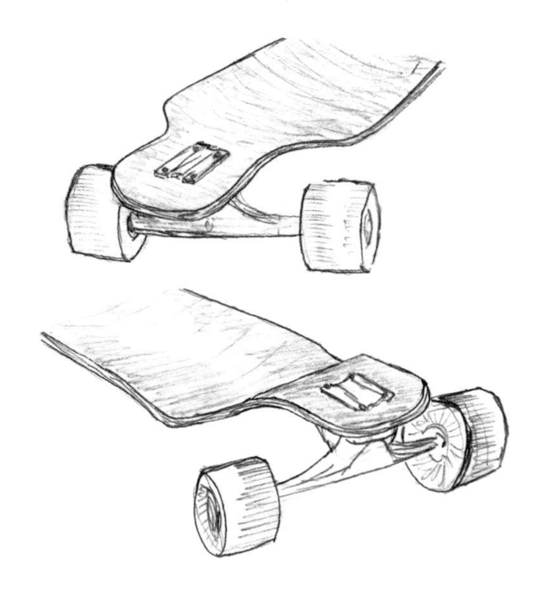

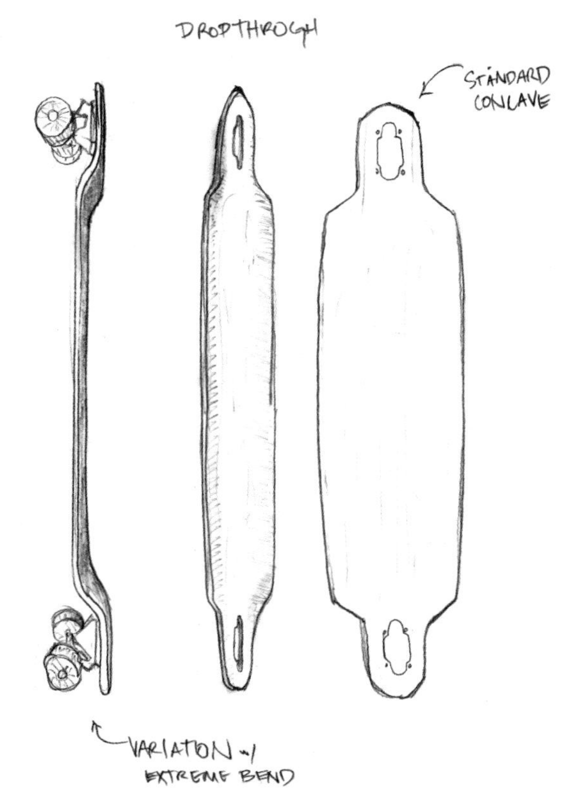

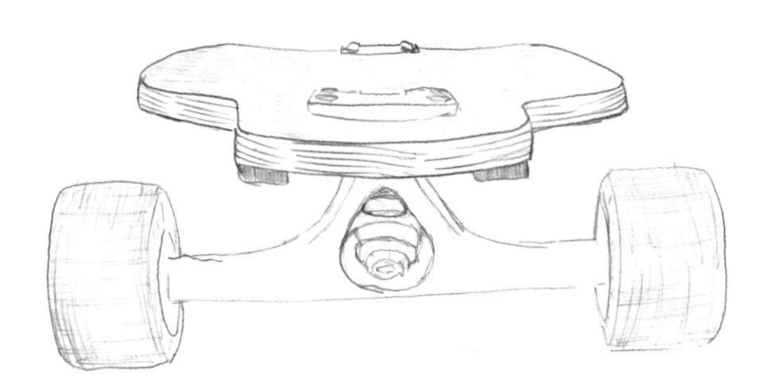

MINIS AND CRUISERS

DESCRIPTION:
Based on the classic plastic banana board decks from the 1970s, these diminutive skateboards are barely big enough to contain two feet, but are designed to provide a fun ride in many of the same situations as a classic longboard cruiser. In the early days of skateboarding, most decks would have been classified as "Minis." It wasn't until the skateboard grew in popularity and function that it also grew in size. Mini skateboards only recently came back into favor when the plastic Penny Board was released in 2010 by an Australian woodworker and skateboard entrepreneur named Ben Mackay. Since then several manufacturers have released throw-back mini decks, often based on reissues of their earliest commercial skateboard products.

SHAPE:
Mini cruisers are short and narrow and mostly flat with a hard bend at the kicktail. The shape is somewhere between a longboard and a street deck. Because these decks don't have widespread appeal, they also don't come in many different shapes and sizes.

RIDER PROFILE:
Mini decks are small, so the smaller and lankier the rider, the better. That limits the ridership mostly to kids. But the small size of the boards also makes them super portable for larger people who want a deck to get around town. These decks are easy to stow away in your backpack, making them popular among the student set, and perfect solutions when you want to do a mix of walking, skating, and taking the bus. Junior high kids prefer them because they fit perfectly in a half-sized locker.

USES:
Mini decks are great entry-level skateboards for little kids getting started in the sport. The big, soft wheels and prominent kicktail make them easy to ride and control. For bigger riders, they are suitable for getting around town and are agile and responsive for dodging dogs and pedestrians. And while not optimized for it, they can be used to do some basic skateboarding tricks and traversing basic road obstacles.

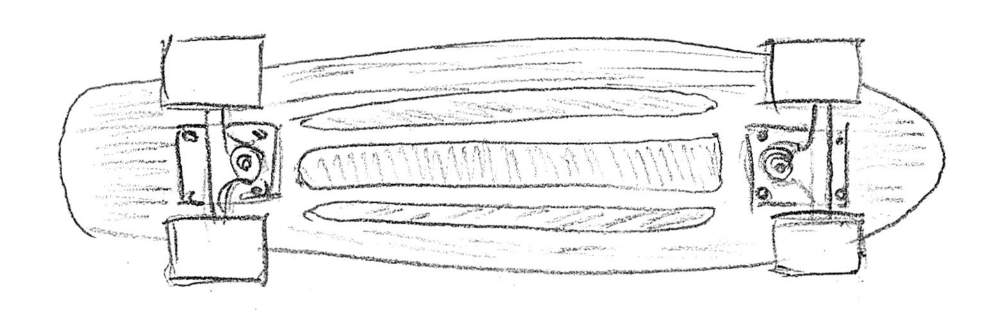

CONSTRUCTION NOTES:

The vast majority of mini decks sold on the market are made from plastic and produced with an injection mold. Plastic mini decks don't have grip tape and instead have a textured surface that gives your feet something to grip. The bottom of a plastic deck is also textured with plastic "ribs" to give the deck extra strength without increasing the overall thickness of the plastic. Some mini decks are constructed from solid wood, or laminated from layers of veneer similar to a standard skateboard or longboard deck.

DIMENSIONS:

These little guys are small, anywhere from 22-in. to 28 in. long. by 4½-in. to 6-in. wide.

WHEEL SIZE:

Despite their small size, they benefit from big, soft wheels just like a classic longboard. The gold standard Penny wheel has a 59 mm diameter and hardness rating of 78a.

WHEEL SPAN:

These short decks also have a super short wheel span, about 9 in.

TRUCK SIZE:

Mini skateboards require specialty trucks that can be hard to find off-the-shelf as these decks are mostly sold complete. The standard Penny truck measures 4 in. wide.

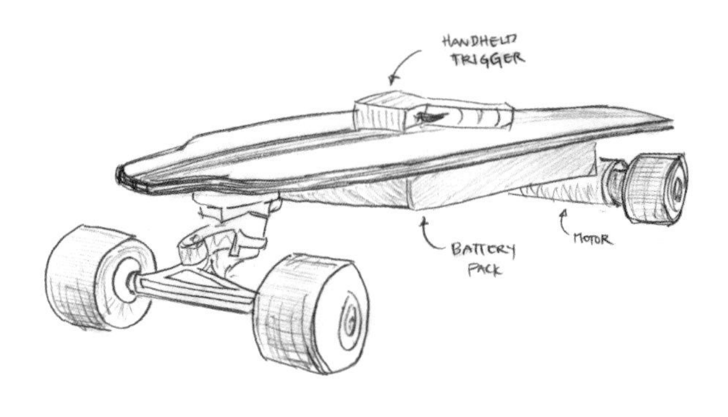

CUSTOM AND ELECTRIC

DESCRIPTION:

Various makers around the U.S.—and many in Southern California—have taken the art of skateboard making to the extreme with a variety of custom shapes and features. Brands like Carver and Arbor and Gravity Boards have been experimenting with specialty decks and trucks in ways that have transformed the sport. But the innovation hasn't stopped there. A new wave of skateboard entrepreneurs are taking the deck in wild new directions

One of the first variations of this kind was the development of the off-road skate deck, with giant all-terrain wheels for extreme downhill riding. Around Southern California another innovation has emerged over the past decade: the paddle longboard, which incorporates a long flexible pole with a rubber ball at the end that's used to propel, steer, and slow the board.

But perhaps the most groundbreaking innovation in skate making history is the introduction of the electric-powered motor. While many skaters balk at the idea of powering a skateboard with something other than your feet, the concept is taking off with young urban commuters. In the past few years, a handful of electric skateboard startups have come onto the scene, using crowdfunding sites like Kickstarter to get their products to the masses.

One of the first to go the electric route is ZBoard, a Southern California-based startup with an engineered deck that can travel about 5 miles at a top speed of 15 mph on a single charge. To operate the deck, the rider moves forward and backward by stepping on front and rear foot pads. More recently, a team of engineers from Silicon Valley came up with the lightweight electric-powered Boosted board, which uses a handheld remote to accelerate and brake.

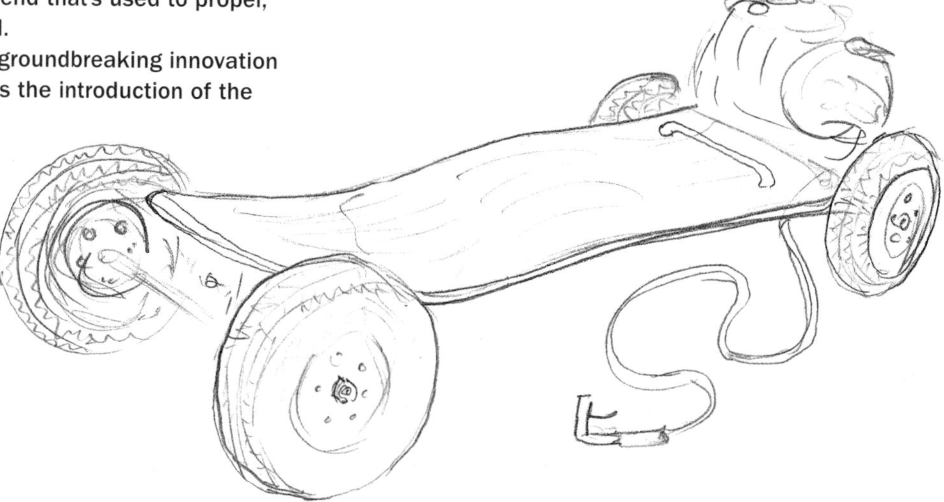

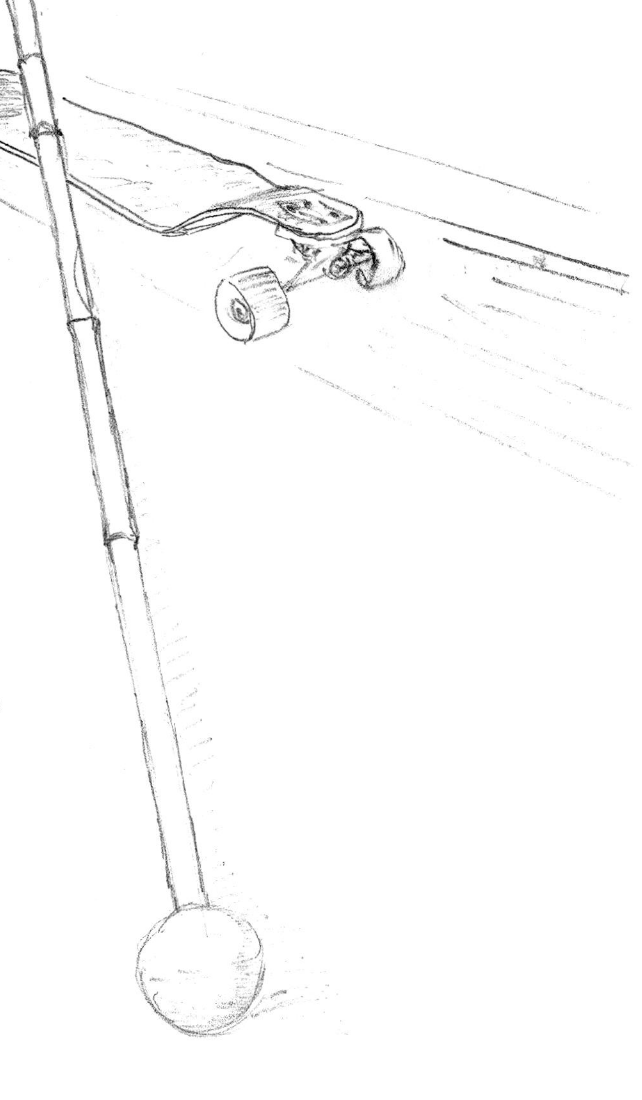

SHAPE:
Custom and electric skate decks don't always look like standard skateboards since they are often designed for specialty uses that require unique shapes, modified components and—in the case of electric skateboards—a place to mount a battery and motor. But if you strip these decks of all their extras, typically you will find a traditional laminated skateboard deck underneath the bells and whistles. The contours are mostly for strength and balance since these decks aren't built for doing tricks or maneuvering rough road conditions.

RIDER PROFILE:
Because this class of skateboard is so diverse, so is the ridership. When it comes to custom longboards and specialty skate decks, riders are typically enthusiasts aiming to push the limits of the traditional skateboard. These are usually riders who want to do something new and different—like ride a skateboard down a dirt bike trail—and have to come up with their own modifications to meet their needs. But the market for electric skateboards is expanding the audience to include newbies and urban commuters who are more interested in a low-cost alternative commute than living the skater lifestyle.

USES:
Again, there are so many variations in the custom skateboard category that the uses vary greatly. Off-road paddle skateboarding is more about long-distance riding since the pole allows the rider to use their upper body strength—in addition to their legs—to propel them up and down hills.

DIMENSIONS:
Off-road skate decks and those used for paddle skateboarding follow similar dimensions as classic longboards and downhill skateboards. The new electric decks, meanwhile, are a lot bigger and heavier.

WHEEL SIZE:
Wheels in this category are typically specialty items that you won't find at your local skateshop. They range in diameter from 2 in. to as much as 6 in. and can clock in at as much as 4 in. wide.

WHEEL SPAN:
Variable depending on the size of the deck.

TRUCK SIZE:
Similar to the wheels, specialty skateboard trucks usually have to be custom ordered, and their size depends on the use.

TRUCK AND WHEEL ASSEMBLIES

The only parts you can't make by hand

THE BASIC SETUP

The preferred setup for a street-ready skate deck includes 8-in.-wide skate trucks, hard and small wheels, precision bearings, thin rubber risers, and ⅞ in.-long hardware. Pick and chose your parts from dozens of top-quality brands.

PRIMER ON SKATE TRUCKS

Unfortunately, DIY manufacturing has still not caught up to the requirements of making steel skateboard trucks, or urethane wheels, or ball bearings, or machine-cut screws and locking nuts. You'll need to buy those at a skateshop before your deck is complete and ready to ride. In the skateboard business, the truck assembly is where all the money is. These setups can run anywhere from 75 bucks for a entry-level setup to as much as $200 for top-of-the-line parts.

Skateboard trucks are the central component of a skateboard deck and contain the main mechanics that allow a rider to maneuver and propel across earth and terrain. There are several elements that make up a skateboard truck.

BASEPLATE

Trucks mount to a skate deck with four screws (the mounting hardware) that pass through a flat base plate with machine-drilled holes. There are two common hole patterns that manufacturers follow, the bigger of which is most common on longboard decks.

KINGPIN

The baseplate connects to a large bolt called the kingpin that does all the work when you turn a skateboard deck. Where the kingpin attaches to the baseplate, it sits in a rubber cup that allows the board to pivot when you lean to turn left or right during a ride.

HANGER

The other end of the kingpin attaches to the hanger. This is the main T-shaped body of the truck. On a street deck, the hanger takes the biggest beating as it grinds up against curbs and railings and other obstacles. It's also the heaviest component. Some manufacturers use expensive alloys that are durable and lighter than steel.

continued...

TRUCK AND WHEEL ASSEMBLIES *continued*

LONGBOARD TRUCKS ARE DIFFERENT

Because of the riding conditions and the size of the deck, longboard trucks have a different configuration of parts than shortboard trucks. The kingpin points in the other direction and has a second pivot point on the front, which allows for better turning on boards with long and wide wheel spans. At left an array of trucks, for small Penny decks all the way up to the longest longboards.

BUSHINGS

Two rubber bushings are sandwiched between the metal parts along the kingpin to pad the truck as it twists and turns. Bushings come in a variety of hardness for different riding conditions. Heavy riders or technical riders often benefit from harder bushings that provide more resistance to sharp impacts. Softer bushings are great for cruising and carving because they require less effort when leaning into a turn.

AXLE

The last piece is the hanger shaft or axle, which extends through the hanger and connects the wheels. The axle is also how skateboard trucks are measured—for instance, probably the most common truck on earth, the Indie 129, measures 129 mm end to end.

When picking out your trucks, you determine the appropriate axle length by measuring the width of the deck. Wide longboards need a bigger axle length. These offer a more stable ride but mean the board is going to take much wider turns. A narrower axle on a street deck allows for sharper turns. The general rule is that the axle length should put the wheels within ¼ in. of the deck's edge. . . but, rules are made to be broken.

The axle height determines the clearance of the deck above the ground. The bigger diameter wheels on a longboard require more clearance and ergo a higher axle height. Street decks have small-diameter wheels and can lie lower to the ground.

pro tip

ADJUST YOUR TRUCKS WITH A SKATE TOOL

Another couple of settings you'll need to adjust on your trucks are the kingpin tightness and height. This is such a common task that someone went and invented an all-purpose tool just for it called a "skate tool." A skate tool has a socket wrench for tightening your wheels on the axle, and a Phillips head screwdriver for tightening the mounting hardware. It also has a larger socket wrench for tightening and adjusting the height of the kingpin.

TRUCK AND WHEEL ASSEMBLIES *continued*

A WHEEL FOR ANY OCCASION
As seen here, skateboard wheels come in a wide variety of colors, shapes, and sizes, from the giant off-road longboard wheels designed for navigating dirt, to the small wheels built for sidewalks and skateparks.

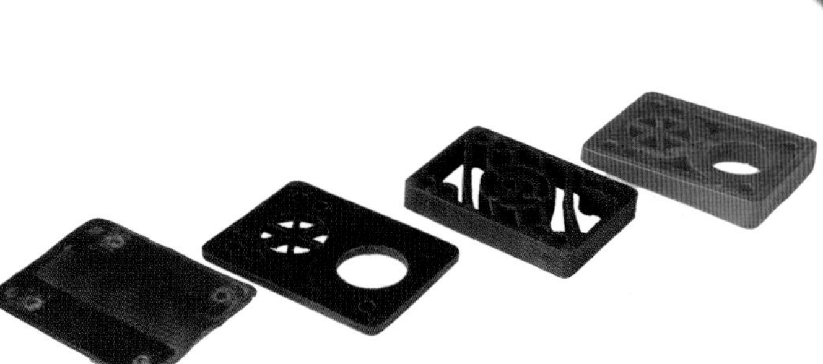

RISE TO THE OCCASION
Risers do exactly what you'd expect—raise the board up off the trucks. They offer cushion during a ride and keep the wheels from rubbing as you corner to prevent wheel bite. Risers are available in a wide range of thicknesses.

THE HARDWARE
The screws and nuts that attach the trucks to the skate deck are a standard 8 mm with a cone-shaped head. Their length varies based on the thickness of the riser.

WHEELS

Modern skateboard wheels have come a long way since the clay and metal wheels of the early days. Wheels are categorized by diameter and hardness, and they vary depending on use. The bigger and softer the wheel the more forgiving they will be when rolling over rocks and cracks and other hazards. That's why you find these on longboards and cruisers in sizes ranging from 67 mm to 80 mm. The smaller and harder the wheel, the better it is for shredding sidewalks and skateparks. A typical street deck features wheels from 52 mm to 58 mm.

HARDWARE

The screws and locking nuts that attach the truck assembly to a skateboard deck are referred to simply as "the hardware." They all measure a standard diameter (8 mm) and thread pattern (10/32). The length you choose depends on the total thickness of your setup, particularly the riser pad. They typically range from 7/8-in. to 1 1/4-in. long.

RISERS

If you need a little extra height to your deck you can add a riser between the truck baseplate and the deck. Risers are essentially rectangular pieces of plastic or rubber, drilled with the same screw holes as your trucks and deck. They come in different thicknesses to accommodate different height needs and can absorb some shock and vibration during a bumpy concrete ride. Risers are one store-bought component that can be swapped out with a DIY solution. I've improvised with salvaged plastic and rubber, and even leather. (Wood risers are not advised.) In addition to raising the board, risers also help protect the wood deck from the harsh metal truck.

BEARINGS

Skateboard wheels spin so well on trucks thanks to precision bearings, which fit inside each skateboard wheel joining it to the axle. When it comes to purchasing skateboard bearings, the more you spend the better your wheels will spin. High performance ceramic bearing are the most expensive. And with good reason. They absorb heat from the friction of a fast-spinning wheel and keep you going fast. One step down are precision steel bearings, followed by plain old steel bearings. Make sure you avoid cheap decks that use anything less than precision steel bearings.

BEARINGS KEEP YOU ROLLING

Bearings come in one-size-fits-all, but they range in quality. Precision steel bearings are the standard. Upgrade to ceramic for high-speed conditions. Avoid inexpensive, standard steel ball bearings.

SET UP YOUR DECK LIKE A PRO: A LESSON FROM STEVE BADILLO

So you've built your deck and it's almost ready to ride. The last step is to apply grip tape and install the trucks and wheels. For a pro lesson on the task, I turned to Steve Badillo, one of Southern California's top pro skaters and a pro teacher of the art and craft of skateboarding.

Badillo made a name for himself riding for team Alva in the 1990s mastering all the tricks in the book. Then he wrote some, publishing the six-book series *Skateboarding: Legendary Tricks*, a collection of tutorials and history lessons on the best skateboarding tricks of all time.

Badillo has earned a reputation as the go-to pro for Hollywood producers looking to infuse a movie or television show with some authentic skateboard culture. In 2005, Badillo played Ty Page in the movie *Lords of Dogtown* with Heath Ledger and Emile Hirsch. Behind the scenes, he helped train the film's lead actors on how to skate like Tony Alva and Stacy Peralta. He continues to get called on for commercials and stunt doubles, and every now and then a lesson for a Barney like me.

I met up with Badillo in Simi Valley at Skatelabs to see his technique for applying grip tape. In his lifetime, Badillo has set up thousands of decks. In this photo series, he shares his foolproof method from start to finish.

1 STICK-TUITIVENESS
Apply grip tape like a pro. Start by peeling off the protective back from the grip tape to reveal the sticky surface.

EIGHT EASY STEPS FOR APPLYING GRIP TAPE

2 CUT DESIGNS IN YOUR GRIP
Before you get started, now's the time to make any stencil cuts or patterns in your grip. Freehand or use a stencil to draw letters, patterns, or pictures in your grip tape ahead of time. Cut from the back with a utility knife or laser cutter.

3 POSITION THE GRIP TAPE
With the back peeled off, position the grip tape over the deck just where you want it. Hover while you make sure it is aligned and centered.

4 STICK FROM ONE END...
Begin applying the grip from one end of the deck, crawling your fingers down the board to press the grip to the deck as you go. Your challenge is to avoid wrinkles and air bubbles.

5 ...TO THE OTHER
If you properly align the grip tape from the start and take your time while sticking it to the deck it should spread smoothly across the length of the board.

6 BURNISH THE EDGE BEFORE CUTTING
Establish a cutting line on your grip tape by running the shaft of an old file or screwdriver along the edge of your deck to burnish an edge. Keep the burnisher at a constant angle as you mark all the way around the deck.

continued...

EIGHT EASY STEPS FOR APPLYING GRIP TAPE *continued*

pro tip

GRIP TAPE

The top surface of a skateboard is covered in grip tape to help you stay afoot while riding. Most grip is sold in sheets or rolls. Your options for grip go way beyond the standard jet black. Grip manufacturers now supply all sorts of colors, patterns, and screen print designs—from clear grip to printed patterns. If you prefer to skip grip tape altogether, you can sprinkle silicon carbide dust (the raw ingredients for making sandpaper) over the top surface during the application of finish so that it dries with a clear grip surface.

7 CUT WITH A UTILITY BLADE
Cut along the marked line from the underside with a razor blade. Hold the blade against the edge of the deck at a consistent angle all the way around for an even edge. Long continuous cuts produce cleaner edges.

8 FINISH THE EDGE
Use a scrap piece of grip tape to sand down the perimeter of the deck and smooth out the edge of the grip.

Q&A WITH STEVE BADILLO

pro-file

MATT BERGER: When did you start skating and how did you get into it?

STEVE BADILLO: I started skateboarding when I was 10 years old when I visited my cousin's house in Orange County. I found an old 1970s wood skateboard in the bushes with a picture of a sunset on the top. I pulled it out of the bushes, tried it out, and asked my cousin if I could have it. I lived on top of a hill, so when I took it home I started bombing the hill. A lot of times I'd go barefoot and sit on the board and butt-bomb the hill.

From 10 years old to 12 years old skateboarding was just fun for me; I wasn't serious about it. Then when I was 12 I got my first professional skateboard from a skateshop and that's when I realized I wanted to be serious about it. The board was a Powell-Peralta Rat Bones deck. I tried to learn a trick a day on that board.

MB: What was your favorite deck to ride at the time? How about of all time?

SB: In the mid '80s when I was learning to skate I had different boards from different companies: Powell-Peralta, Santa Cruz, Hosoi Skateboards, Madrid, and Sims. But in 1989 I got sponsored by Alva skateboards and rode on an Alva board for the next 19 years. Then in 2008 I left Alva and started skateboarding for Skip Engblom and Santa Monica Airlines skateboards.

My favorite board of all time was the first board I bought: the Rat Bones board with Rat Bones wheels and Tracker trucks. That's the board that inspired me to be better.

MB: Since you started riding, what are some of the most important innovations to the skateboard and why?

SB: In the '80s skateboards came in different shapes so we got to skate a bunch of different boards to find out which shape we liked. That was fun back then. Shapes like the hammerhead, tri-tails, square tails, money bumps, deep concaves.

And then in the late '80s the first boards with a kick nose came out and skateboarding had an evolution with the kick nose. New tricks could be done and the tricks got bigger. At the same time the kick nose came out, street skating got a lot bigger. The boards started to become symmetrical—what we call the popsicle shape—with a round tail and a round nose.

MB: What do you think is the next big thing in the evolution of the skateboard deck?

SB: What's the next big thing in skateboarding evolution? Well the next big thing has already been happening for the last 10 years, which is that skateboards are now going back to shapes influenced by decks from the '70s and '80s. The boards have modern concaves with old school shapes. But the main manufacturers of skateboards are still the popsicle stick shape.

CHAPTER 3

HOW TO BUILD A HACKBOARD

If your grandpa rode a skateboard when he was a kid, it was probably hacked together similar to the deck in this first project.

It might be hard to believe, but your skateboarding grandpa was probably more of a daredevil than you are, because when he bombed a hill, he did it with a heavy plank of oak outfitted with metal or clay wheels that would seize with the tiniest of rocks and send him flying through the air.

Although the materials and parts I'm using for this deck project have improved tremendously since your grandpa was a kid, the process he and his buddies pioneered for slapping together a DIY skateboard deck in a weekend lives on: Start with a plank of wood—found, bought, or borrowed—and cut it to size and shape. Clean up the edges. Drill holes for the trucks. Deck it out with grip tape and your favorite pair of trucks and wheels. Then hit the pavement.

If you're motivated, you can put together a simple hackboard in your garage or even at your kitchen table in an afternoon using mostly scavenged parts. Spend a little more time with it and you can customize the shape or trick it out with your own artwork or a nice wood finish.

A QUICK CLASSIC
Cruise with the best of them on this compact yet roomy deck made from a flat sheet of plywood in less than a weekend.

the goods

TOOLS
Jigsaw, 4-in-1 combination rasp/file, utility knife, sandpaper and hand sanding block, drill-driver with ¼-in. drill-and-countersink bit.

MATERIALS
½-in.-thick Baltic birch plywood, polyurethane wood finish.

EQUIPMENT
Sturdy table or work surface, clamps, foam brush, lint-free rag, dust mask, safety glasses.

SETUP
Skateboard trucks, wheels, bearings, risers, grip tape.

the hackboard

Featuring cutaway fenders and a modified surfboard shape that leaves plenty of room for your Converse high tops, this hackboard makes carving and turning a breeze, whether you're gliding down the Venice Boardwalk or bombing the neighborhood hills.

LENGTH:
32 in.

WIDTH:
8 in.

WHEEL SPAN:
21 ¼ in.

MATERIALS:
½ in. Baltic birch plywood, grip tape

TRUCKS:
Independent 129

RISERS:
⅛ in. plastic risers

BEARINGS:
Bones REDS

WHEELS:
67mm Sector 9

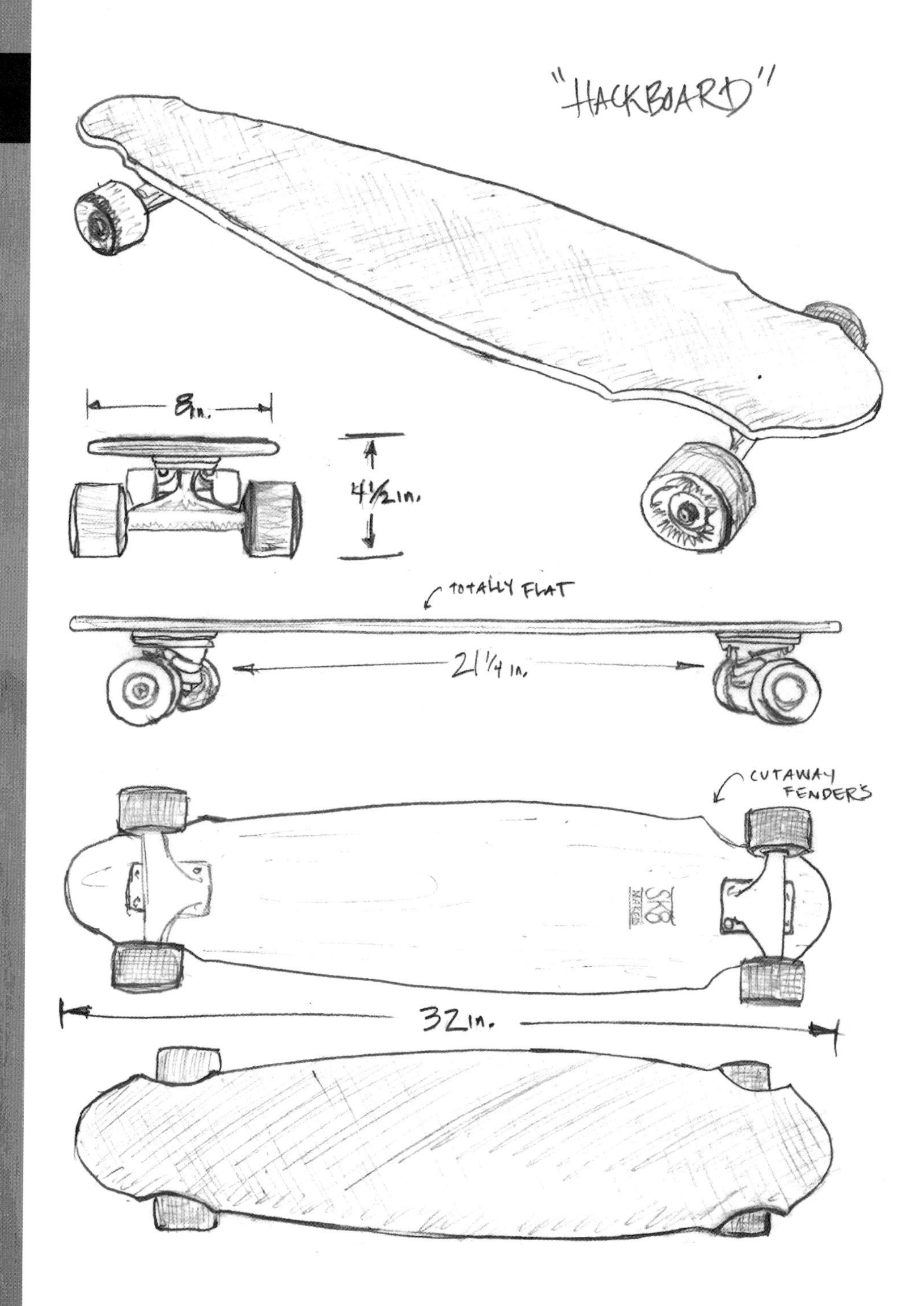

CHOOSE THE RIGHT MATERIAL

You can make a hackboard out of just about anything that's flat and strong enough to hold your weight—an expensive piece of hardwood, free reclaimed building materials—but the choice material for this project is a good quality piece of Baltic birch plywood. You can find the authentic stuff at most local lumber yards and woodworking supply stores.

Superior to the plywood products available at many home centers, Baltic birch plywood is super flat and stable and is great for making things that need to stand up to wear and tear but also look good, like drawers and doors for kitchen cabinets. Baltic birch plywood is typically sold in 5-ft. by 5-ft. sheets, and is not to be confused with standard birch veneer plywood. While the faces of regular birch plywood may look nice enough, the interior plies are of lesser quality and won't hold up to the destructive impact of a skater. Meanwhile, Baltic birch plywood has high-quality inner plies that are free of voids, even in thickness, and look really sharp in profile.

If you want a little flex and bounce in your ride and you don't weigh too much, you can't go wrong with ½-in.-thick Baltic birch plywood. For a sturdier ride, a heavier rider, or a longer deck, upgrade to ¾-in.-thick Baltic birch plywood.

GO FOR THE GOOD STUFF
A step up from the plywood you find at most home centers, Baltic Birch plywood is made up of multiple layers of void-free, quality veneers.

DESIGN A PAPER TEMPLATE

Before you cut into your plywood, the first step is to come up with a deck shape. After a few sketches on a notepad, I like to take my favorite designs full size by creating paper templates. Seeing a life-sized shape can bring out design flaws that are hard to spot on a small thumbnail sketch. A full-size template also allows you to locate the truck holes and any other design elements you'll be adding to your deck.

To make a full-size template, start by marking a dark, straight centerline that's at least the length of your skateboard deck. Then lightly pencil sketch the rough shape of the deck as you imagined it on your sketchpad. Don't add any detail yet, just identify the basic dimensions and curves. Where along the length is the widest point of the board? If you're adding fenders like I did, determine where they should be positioned in relation to the trucks and wheels.

Once you've got the basic shape sketched out, refine one side of the paper template to a final shape. Sharpen the straight lines with a ruler. Fair the curves using various round objects of different diameters, like glass jars and cups. For small-diameter circles, things like soda bottle tops and tape dispensers work great.

TOOLS FOR LAYOUT AND DESGIN
To determine the shape of your deck, start by creating a paper template. Draw a centerline, and use a variety of measuring and marking tools to design one half of the deck shape. Use round objects like bottles or rolls of tape to help you draw perfect curves of different diameters. A plastic riser comes in handy for positioning the skateboard trucks.

CUT OUT THE SHAPE

With one side of your template complete, fold the paper in half and cut along the line with scissors or a utility knife.

REFINE THE DESIGN (far right)

When you unfold the template after cutting, your completed deck shape is revealed. To refine the template, fold it again and trim the template evenly on both sides.

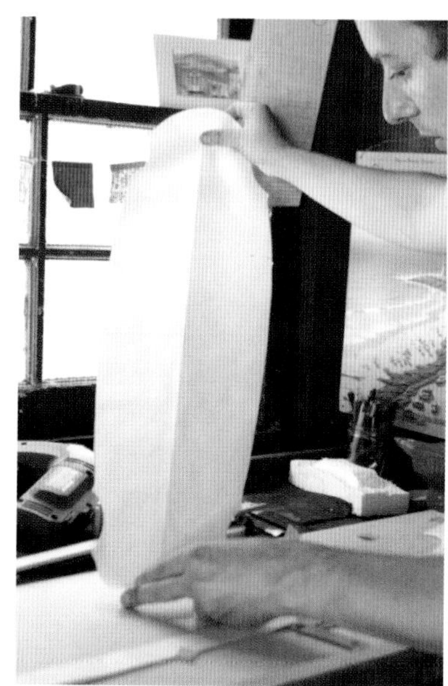

PUT THE TEMPLATE TO WORK

Transfer the template shape to your piece of plywood. Tape it in place and trace with a pencil.

When you think you've got the shape just right, fold the template in half down the centerline. Then grab a pair of scissors or a utility knife and cut out the shape carefully, cutting both sides of the fold at once. When you unfold the paper, like making paper dolls, your final deck shape is revealed.

If you don't like what you see, you can trim it or make refinements; Just make sure you fold the template back in half to maintain symmetry by trimming both sides evenly.

Finally, transfer your design to your deck material and get ready to saw some wood!

HOW TO MAKE CLEAN CUTS WITH A JIGSAW

A hackboard by its very nature is the least expensive approach to building a skateboard deck. So you can follow a similar approach in the choice of tools you use to make one. Enter the jigsaw, probably the least expensive, most versatile wood cutting power tool worth keeping around the garage. A jigsaw can cut a straight line or a curvy one; it's easy to handle no matter your skill level; it's relatively safe; and it's pretty cheap if you don't need all the bells and whistles. If you don't have a jigsaw of your own and aren't ready to spring for one, chances are you can borrow one from the guy down the street who hangs out in his garage all weekend. With DIYers, they're easy to come by.

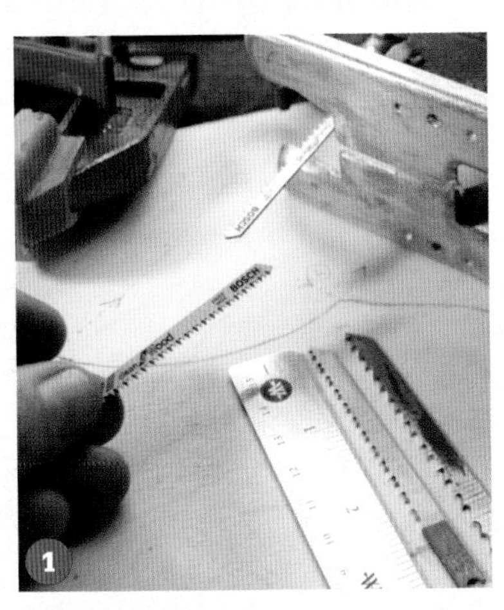

1 CHOOSE THE RIGHT BLADE
To avoid splintering and chip-out when cutting with a jigsaw, choose a sharp, wood-cutting blade. The optimal size is between 14 teeth per inch (TPI) and 20 TPI. The higher the number, the finer the cut.

2 STEADY YOUR WORK
A jigsaw vibrates like nobody's business when it's running, so take time to secure the skateboard deck to a sturdy table or sawhorse with clamps. Apply even downward pressure and make sure you don't push the tool faster than the blade can cut. Your job is to guide the way.

3 LEAVE A LITTLE WIGGLE ROOM
Cut just close enough to the line so that you don't cross it, but not so far that you have a ton of material to remove later. As much as 1⁄16 in. can be removed easily with handtools.

4 RELIEF CUTS FOR SHARP TURNS
When cutting sharp turns or tight curves with a jigsaw, relief cuts save the day. These strategically placed incisions give your blade an easy place to exit the cut when things get dicey.

MASTER THE JIGSAW

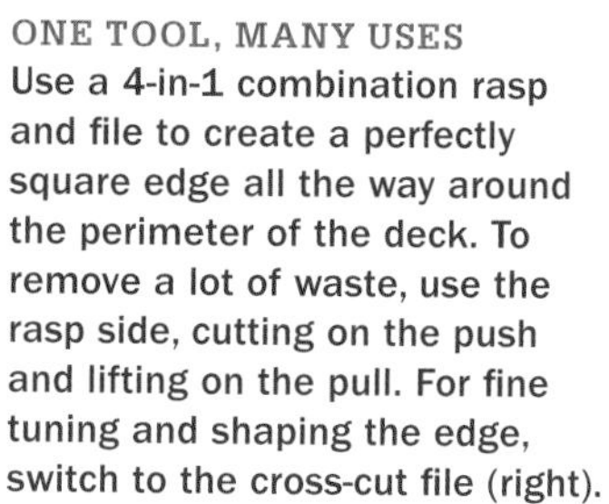

ONE TOOL, MANY USES
Use a 4-in-1 combination rasp and file to create a perfectly square edge all the way around the perimeter of the deck. To remove a lot of waste, use the rasp side, cutting on the push and lifting on the pull. For fine tuning and shaping the edge, switch to the cross-cut file (right).

SHAPE THE EDGE WITH A RASP AND FILE

This the second time in this book that I'm going to ask you to buy a tool that you didn't even know you needed. But it turns out that a 4-in-1 combination rasp and file is one of the slickest cutting tools in a skatemaker's shop. A rasp is to wood what an eraser is to paper. It gives you plenty of control to quickly remove material as you shape. It also works faster and creates less dust than hand sanding.

Rasps and files come in a variety of sizes, cutting patterns, and contours. Rasps, the most aggressive cutters of the lot, have a surface covered with sharp metal teeth that bite into the wood on each pass. Files are much less aggressive and use parallel rows of low teeth to gnaw away at wood.

The tool I'm using is a combination 4-in-1 rasp-file with one flat surface and one half-round surface. Each side is split between a cross-cut file for fine finish work, and a sawtooth rasp for removing lots of material quickly.

The round side of the tool is great for shaping inside and outside curves, like those on the fenders of my deck design. The flat side, meanwhile, is used to smooth out the long flat sections of the deck.

It's hard to tell by looking at it, but a rasps and files only cut in one direction, and it's generally best to cut on the push stroke. On the pull stroke back to starting position, lift the tool slightly to prevent the teeth from contacting your material.

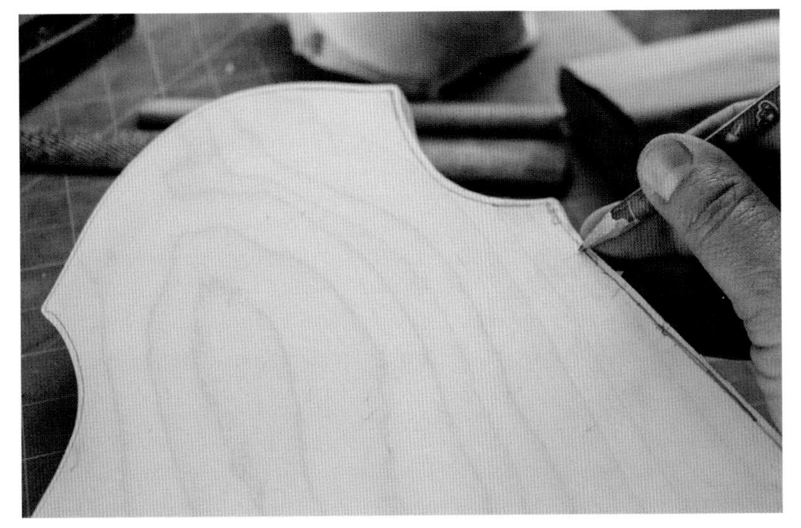

START WITH A GUIDELINE (left)
Mark a line on the top and bottom face of the skateboard deck about ⅛ in. from the edge. Rest your middle finger on the freshly filed edge of the deck, and hold your pencil steady as you mark a continuous line all the way around.

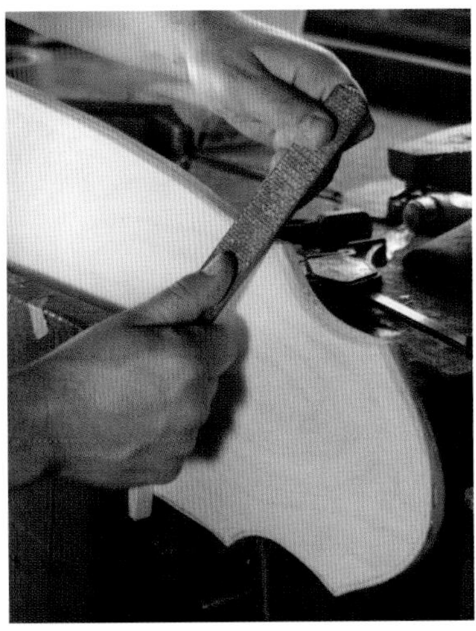

ROUND IT OFF
Create a rounded edge on both sides of the skateboard deck with your 4-in-1 combination rasp and file. Work the sharp edge to the line, keeping the curve consistent.

SQUARE UP THE EDGE BEFORE YOU ROUND IT

Before you start chomping away at your edge, you want to first refine the shape cut with the jigsaw so that you have a square edge all the way around the perimeter of the deck. Hold the tool at a perfect 90° to the surface of the deck. Then make long sweeping cuts. Do this first with the rasp side of the tool, then make a final finish pass with the file side.

Remove any bumps, dips, dents, or nicks until there's a smooth continuous edge all around. What your eyes can't see, your fingers can. Run your hand along the edge to identify any microscopic flaws that a visual once-over won't reveal. Or don't . . . if you plan on thrashing your deck post haste.

Once you're satisfied with the shape and the edge is square to the top and bottom surface, move on to rounding over the edge. First, run a pencil line about ⅛ in. from the edge all the way around the deck on both faces. This marks the maximum distance you'll cut, and you'll use it as a guide as you shape.

Next, hold the tool 45° to the deck and cut a hard bevel all the way around the edge. Then round the bevel by filing down the hard edge, alternating between rasp and file for rough and fine cuts.

Finally, hand sand all surfaces and edges to a final finish. If you've removed all the big flaws with your file, you can start with 120-grit sandpaper and progress through each successive grit until you reach 220 grit. That's fine enough for applying a wood finish. Sand in the direction of the grain, not against it.

SAND IT SMOOTH
Finish up the deck by sanding the entire surface with a sanding block. After filing the edge, start with 120-grit sandpaper. Increase the grit to 150, 180, and 220 to prep the surface for a finish.

skate school

HOW TO DRILL PERFECT TRUCK HOLES

You can put all the effort in the world into building the perfect deck and then ruin it for good by doing a lousy job drilling the holes for the trucks. This is an important task—if you drill your holes off by even a fraction of an inch, the trucks won't fit or the alignment will be off, causing the board to veer from a straight line or wobble excessively. But if you're careful and diligent, you can drill eight accurate holes with a handheld drill driver. Here's how.

Acquire your trucks and wheels before you drill the holes to ensure that they match up. There are two common patterns of truck holes that manufacturers use and you want to make sure you cut the right one. Then just take your time measuring and marking out the layout lines. Be sure to use a sharp pencil.

The most important step in building a high-quality skateboard deck is drilling the holes for the trucks and wheels. Take care to ensure perfect alignment between the front and back trucks. If you're off by even a fraction of an inch, your deck won't ride straight.

1 MEASURE TWICE, CUT ONCE
Marking the location of the skateboard truck holes is the most critical step in the skatemaking process. Draw a centerline and then use it to measure and mark each of the holes.

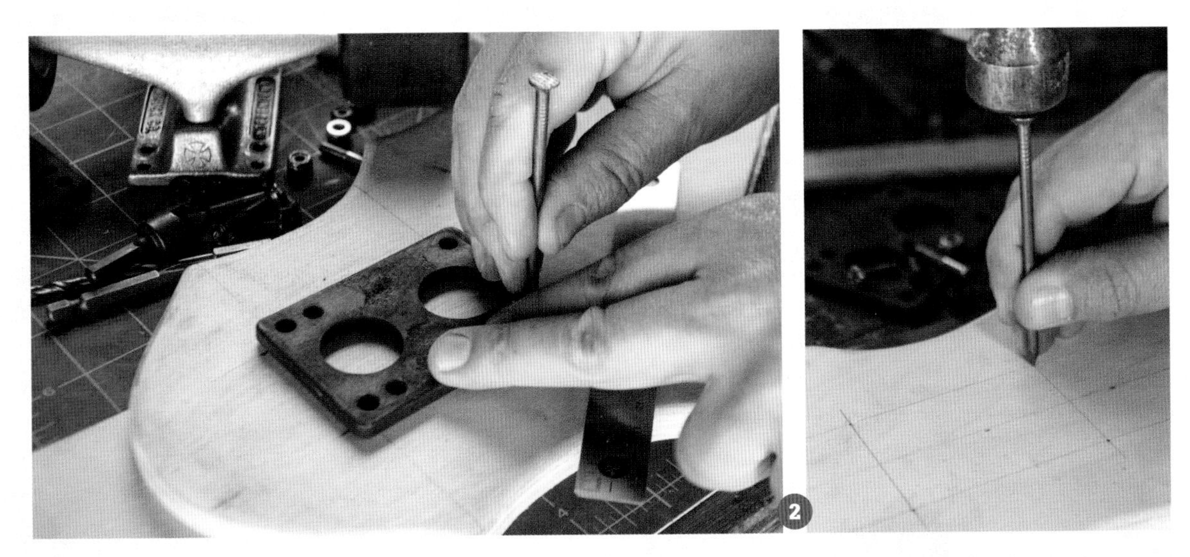

2 MARK THE HOLE
Once your pencil lines are laid out, use a riser pad to double check your work. If the holes line up with your lines, use a nail to mark the center. (above, left) Bang the nail with a hammer to punch a dimple to guide the drill bit. (above, right)

3 SIGHT THE BIT AS YOU CUT
Before you drill into the wood, sight the bit to make sure it's straight. Set up a carpenter's square next to your drill bit and hold the drill steady to keep it parallel to the square as you drill through the wood.

4 CUT A SHALLOW COUNTERSINK
Cut a bevel around the edge of the hole with a special countersink bit, available at most hardware stores. Cut it deep enough so that the truck screws don't stick up from the surface of your deck.

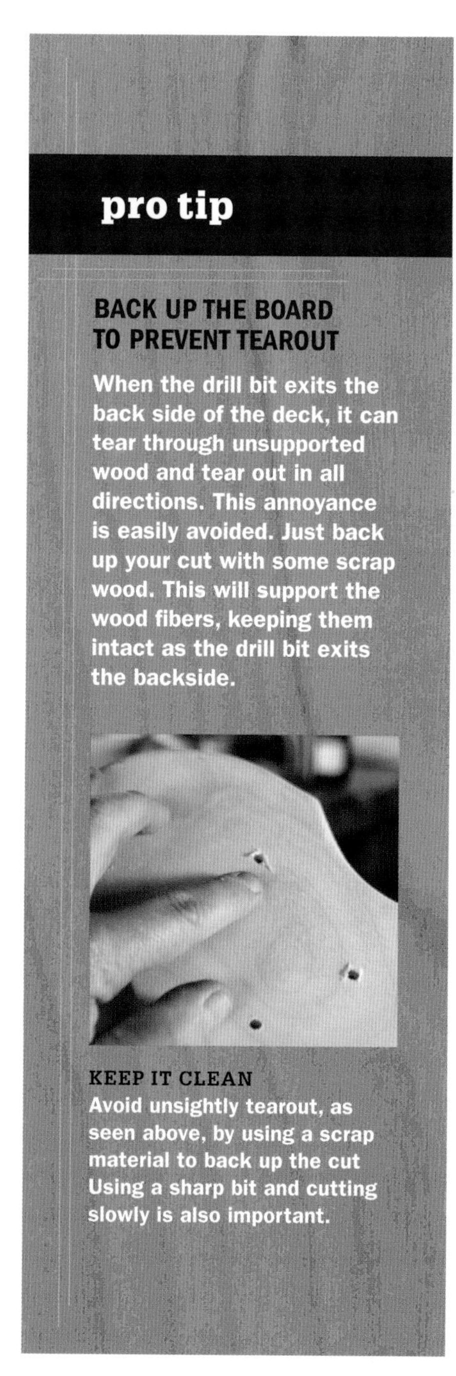

pro tip

BACK UP THE BOARD TO PREVENT TEAROUT

When the drill bit exits the back side of the deck, it can tear through unsupported wood and tear out in all directions. This annoyance is easily avoided. Just back up your cut with some scrap wood. This will support the wood fibers, keeping them intact as the drill bit exits the backside.

KEEP IT CLEAN
Avoid unsightly tearout, as seen above, by using a scrap material to back up the cut Using a sharp bit and cutting slowly is also important.

APPLY A CLEAR COAT FINISH

With the board shaped and the truck holes drilled, you're now ready to finish and weatherproof your deck. This requires applying a few coats of wood finish to the edges and surfaces with a foam brush.

Where I live, in California, many of the best performing woodworking finishes have been banned for home use because of environmental protection laws. You can't even order them online. So lately I've made do with water-based polyurethane or an outdoor spar urethane. Both dry fast into a hard plastic shell and offer good protection against the elements. If you don't live in California, an oil- based polyurethane is the most durable finish you can choose.

A good finish starts with a well-sanded surface. You can achieve this with a handheld sanding block or a palm sander. Starting with 120-grit wet/dry sandpaper and working your way through the various grits until you reach 220-grit. All surfaces—top, bottom, and edges—should be smooth to the touch and free of scratches and tool marks before you apply the finish. You can get a sense of your progress by wiping down the surface with a wet rag.

When you're satisfied with your surface prep, it's time to apply the first coat of finish. I like to start with the top surface. This side of the deck gets covered with grip tape, so it's a great place to practice. If you mess up, no one will see it.

Pour a puddle of finish on the deck and use your brush to spread it evenly across the surface. Take long brush strokes to produce a nice clean surface. If your brush starts to drag or stick, add more finish to lubricate it. When the entire surface is covered—the top and edges—make one more pass across the entire length of the deck and take care to remove random brush strokes. It's also a good idea to check the underside of the deck and clean up any drip marks, particularly at the truck holes and along the edge.

When the top surface is dry to the touch, flip it over and repeat. The more coats of finish you apply, the longer your deck will last.

Between each coat, let the finish dry completely and sand the surface briefly with 320-grit sandpaper to polish it up for the next coat and remove any nibs and specks in the finish. For the final coats, wipe on a thin layer of finish using a lint-free rag or old white T-shirt.

LAY ON THE FINISH
Protect your skateboard deck against weather, wear, and tear by applying a few coats of outdoor urethane finish. Use a a foam brush and apply an even first coat. Use the light to ensure that the entire surface has a shiny reflection.

SAND IT SMOOTH
Between coats of finish, lightly sand the surface with 320-grit or finer sandpaper. This removes any bumps and burrs that appear after the first coat of finish is applied.

pro tip

THREE STEPS TO REPAIR TEAR-OUT

1 ADD A DROP OF GLUE
Apply glue to the splintered piece and the area where it will be applied.

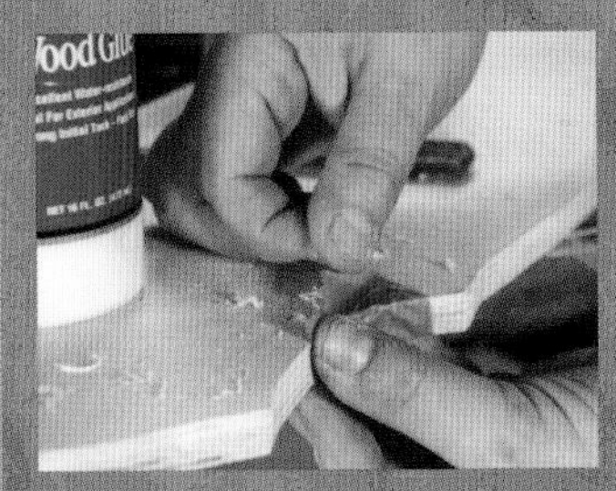

2 TAPE IT DOWN
Tape the splinter firmly in place to hold it while the glue dries. About 30 minutes should do it.

3 MAKE IT DISAPPEAR
Sand the area while the glue is still a little tacky. The glue lines will fill with sawdust and make it almost invisible.

FINAL TOUCHES

When your finish is completely dry and cured according to the manufacturer's recommendation on the back of the can or bottle, you're ready to slap on some grip tape, install the trucks and wheels, and hit the pavement.

Gripping a deck with so many curves is a little more challenging than applying grip tape to a standard street deck, so take your time marking and cutting the tape. I like to apply it oversized and then trim away the waste, as shown in the photos below. For a few tips from a pro, take a look aat "Set Up Your Deck Like a Pro" on page 44.

GIVE IT SOME GRIP
After the finish has set, apply a sheet of grip tape to the top of the deck. Use the long edge of a screwdriver to burnish a line around the deck.

TRIM IT TO SHAPE
Cut out the grip tape with a utility knife blade. Use the burnished line as a guide.

The great thing about hackboards is that you can design them for components you may already have. This deck was designed specifically for a set of trucks and wheels, salvaged from an old Sector 9 longboard from the late 1990s, that I had laying around the house. The trucks are Independent size 129. The wheels are 67mm for plowing over small bumps, dips, and obstacles. The bearings are Bones REDS. What you choose for your own board may vary. And it should. That's the beauty of building a hackboard: Use what you have on hand.

Congratulations, you just built your first skateboard from scratch!

GET READY TO ROLL
Installing the trucks is a breeze if you have the right tools. A cordless driver and a universal skate tool are musts.

pro·file

DISTRICT SKATES

WEBSITE:
districtmillworks.com
&
districtskates.com

SK8MAKER:
Jeremy Williams

WHERE:
Los Angeles, Calif.

FEATURED DECK:
Reclaimed oak pressed deck

In a dusty sprawling workshop and former flour mill in the up-and-coming arts district in downtown Los Angeles, a startup skateboard company is taking root, with big ambitions to build the best decks in the world right here in the U.S. of A.

The guys at District Millworks mostly spend their days building custom interiors for restaurants and retail stores. They also churn out tables and chairs and their trademark product: high-end shuffleboard tables, like the ones you covet in the back room of your favorite local pub.

A few years ago they added custom skate decks to their repertoire. Jeremy Williams is the owner operator at District Millworks and the upstart spinoff, District Skates. He and his guys came up with the idea to press high-quality skatedecks with the best woods and eco-conscious adhesives available. They found a special niche using materials like reclaimed barn wood and salvaged oak railroad ties. The result is an organic, natural deck with all the attributes of a good skateboard.

Two years ago, District Skates upped its game big time when it acquired a collection of enormous two-part hydraulic presses, shapers, drills, and other specialty skateboard manufacturing equipment from the former World Industries, the mega skateboard company that essentially created the modern-day skate manufacturing process in the early 1980s. Williams says the presses were the same ones used a quarter-century ago to press up the first run of decks for the "Godfather of Street Skating," Rodney Mullen.

For now, District Skates sells just a few decks a week, but the team has big plans to put the equipment back into operation full time to supply American-made decks to small skate companies who would rather do business with an eco-conscious company in the U.S. than a mass-market operation in China.

MAKE YOUR MARK
District boards are all marked with their distinct logo.

A PRODUCTION MINDSET
A wall of skate deck presses (below) allows District to build multiple boards at the same time, all to precision specs.

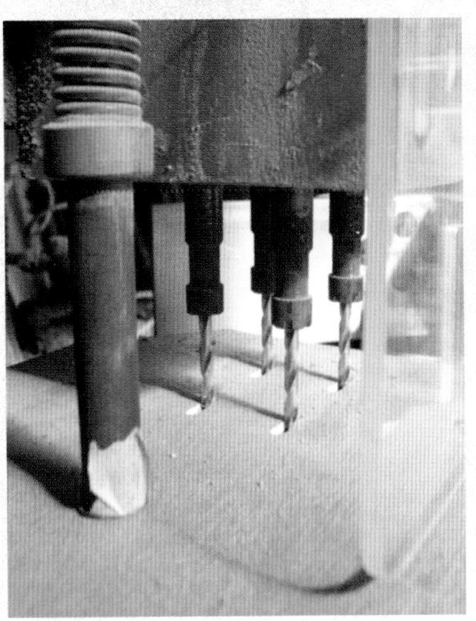

PRECISION IS KEY
A boring machine set up to cut four holes at the same time makes quick work of the truck holes.

BOARDS IN WAITING
Once the decks come off the press, they're racked to await final shaping and refinement.

READY TO ROLL
With trucks and wheels in place, another District Skates board is ready for pavement.

CHAPTER 4

HOW TO BUILD A VINTAGE PINSTRIPED CRUISER

If you want to kick it up a notch from the hackboard in the previous chapter but still use the same basic toolset, upgrade to this classic hardwood "sidewalk surfer" based on real examples from the late 1950s and early 1960s.

For some inspiration when designing the decks covered in this chapter, I took a drive to the Skateboard Hall of Fame in Simi Valley, Calif., where co-owner Todd Huber has amassed an amazing collection of vintage skate decks from classic makers and small shops that have come and gone around Southern California through the decades.

The thing to know about these antique designs is that they are not high-performance decks like the ones you can buy at a modern skateshop. The material choice means these decks are stiff and heavy. But they are fun to make and ride. And decked out with modern trucks and wheels, these little spitfires are great for freestyling, barefoot riding, and just getting around the neighborhood.

Plus you can have a lot of fun mixing and matching wood species to come up with a great design that will turn heads everywhere you take it.

BACK TO THE BEACH
Strips of solid hardwoods edge-glued in a pinstripe pattern make for a vintage look and a solid ride.

the goods

TOOLS
Jigsaw, 4-in-1 combination rasp/file, sander (electric or hand-powered), drill driver, ¼-in. drill bit, countersink bit.

MATERIALS
Hardwood, PVA wood glue, glue brushes, polyurethane wood finish, dust mask, safety glasses.

EQUIPMENT
Sturdy table or work surface, clamps, bench hook, foam brush.

ACCESSORIES
Trucks and wheels (size may vary depending on the size and shape of your finished deck), bearings, risers.

vintage pinstriped skateboard

Inspired by the early 1950s "sidewalk surfer" skateboards, this solid wood deck features cove-shaped fenders and a classic surfboard shape that's comfy on your bare feet and perfect for getting around the neighborhood in style.

LENGTH:
28 in.

WIDTH:
7 ½ in.

WHEEL SPAN:
18 ½ in.

MATERIALS:
White oak, wenge

TRUCKS:
Independent 129

RISERS:
⅛ in. plastic risers

BEARINGS:
Bones REDS

WHEELS:
Powell-Peralta 85A
Rat Bones

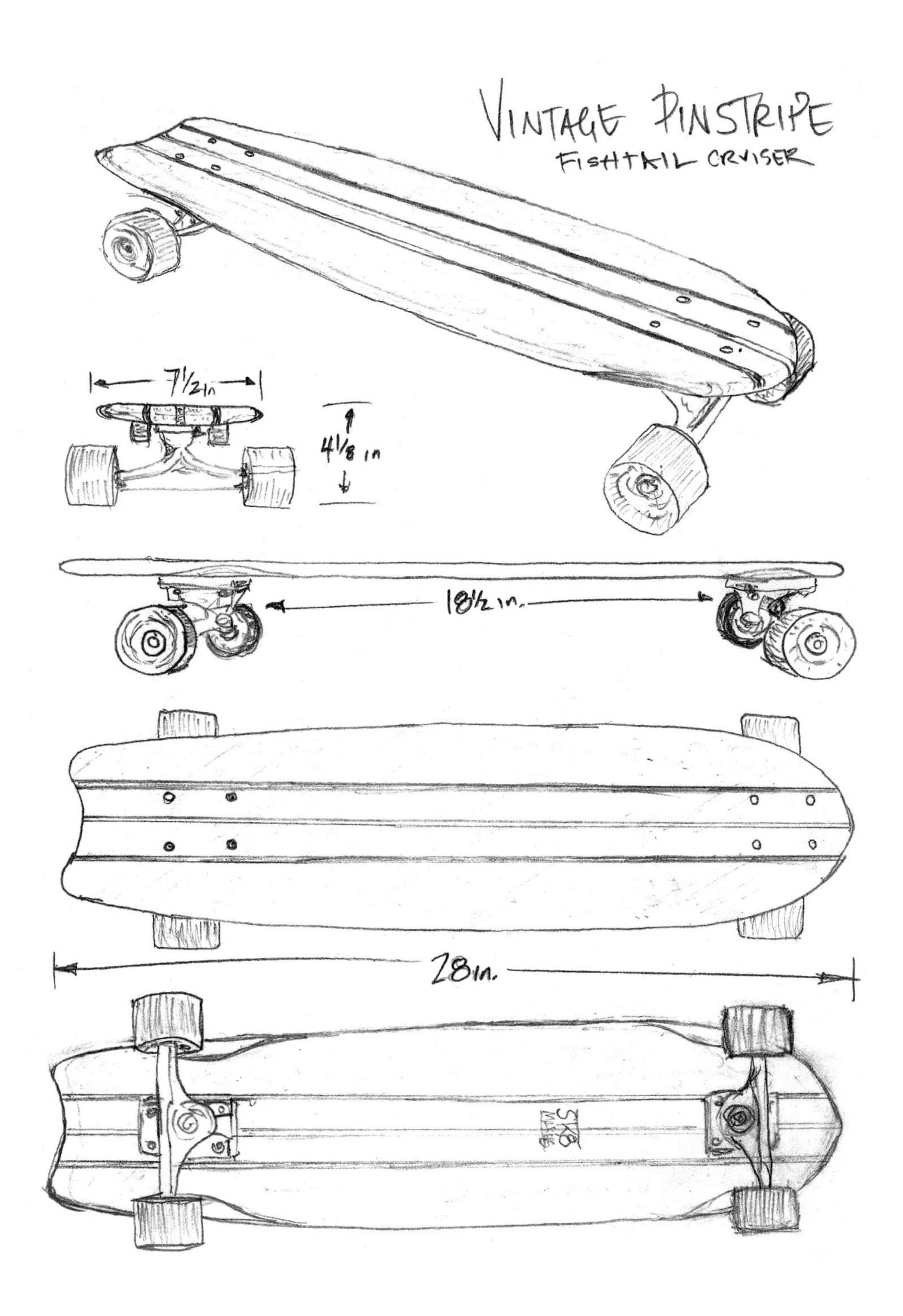

WORKING WITH HARDWOOD LUMBER

While the tools and processes for cutting, shaping, and smoothing this deck are mostly the same as the ones used on the previous hackboard deck, there's one big difference: You'll be working with solid wood instead of plywood, which introduces a few extra challenges.

For starters, beware of sticker shock. The most colorful woods come from the most exotic locations, and the prices for these have skyrocketed in the last decade as a result of overharvesting and poor forest management. When I first started making colorful longboard decks in the mid 1990s, you could find exotic species like wenge or padauk for about seven bucks a board foot. Today, it's more than three times that thanks to dwindling supplies and the increasing cost of transporting big, heavy trees around the world.

Domestic hardwoods like oak, maple, and walnut are much more affordable and in much greater supply. They are ideal for this project.

HALLOWED HARDWOODS

The lumber racks at House of Hardwoods in Culver City, Calif., are stocked with a large variety of domestic and exotic hardwoods, from alder to zebrawood.

THE SCIENCE OF WOOD MOVEMENT

The next important thing to understand about solid wood lumber is this: Wood moves. It shrinks and expands with changes in humidity, and even the strongest glue bond or wood finish isn't going to stop it.

When subjected to dramatic changes in weather conditions (like taking your deck from a rainy day in Seattle to a hot, dry day in New Mexico), wood moves. If you don't take a few precautions to control that movement when choosing your materials and preparing the wood parts during the build, your material will twist, warp, bend, and generally misbehave. Those are bad things for a skateboard.

The first step in battling wood movement is to seek out the straightest boards when you go shopping for lumber. Only buy pieces that are straight and square and discard the pieces that are twisted or warped. Inspect each board thoroughly, and leave the warped or twisted ones for the next guy who wasn't smart enough to read this book.

Next, keep your lumber stored in a temperate, dry place that doesn't experience big changes in humidity or temperature. And let the wood acclimate to the conditions in your workshop for a few days before you start cutting into it.

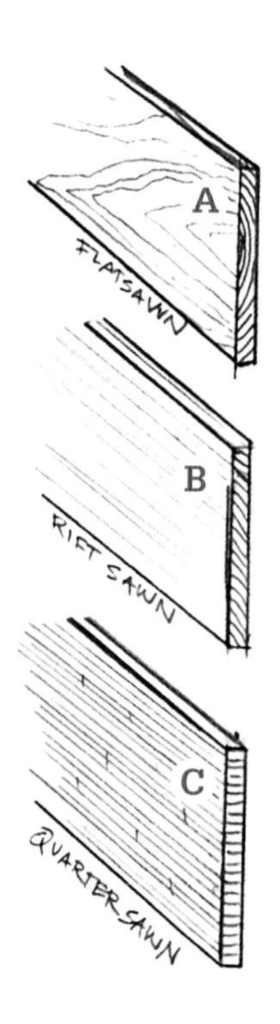

Finally, study the wood grain. With practice, you can tell a lot about how stable the wood is based on the orientation of the rings and how they appear on each face of a board. The diagram at left shows a cross section of a tree with the growth rings radiating from the center. Like a butcher's chart showing cuts of meat on a cow, this diagram shows the cuts of wood in a log: Flatsawn, riftsawn, and quartersawn. You can identify the type of cut by examining the end grain and face grain patterns on a piece of wood. Some are a mix of two or more types.

Flatsawn and mixed sawn lumber are the most common cuts you'll find while shopping at a home center or hardware store. The growth rings on these boards appear on the end grain as rainbows and on the edge and wide faces as cathedrals. Flatsawn wood is the least stable cut and is prone to twisting and warping.

Quartersawn lumber is at the other end of the spectrum; It is the most stable cut, but it's less common and more expensive. The grain runs straight up and down the thickness of the board. On the face, it appears in straight, parallel lines along the length of a board; on the edges, you see flatsawn peaks. Lumber mills waste a lot of material preparing quartersawn lumber, contributing to its high price.

The growth rings on riftsawn lumber appear in a diagonal pattern on the end grain, creating the much sought-after straight-line pattern on both the face and the edge. This also makes it the most stable cut of all, meaning that it shrinks and swells less than the other cuts.

START WITH SQUARE, STRAIGHT LUMBER

Hardwood lumber seldom comes cut to the exact dimensions you'll need for your custom deck. There's a whole series of operations required to mill rough lumber to its final width, thickness, and length, and keep it straight with square corners. The best combination of tools for this operation is the bandsaw, tablesaw, planer, and jointer.

If you don't have any of these machines, team up with someone who does—either a skilled woodworker buddy who can do all the cutting for you, or pay a premium at the lumber yard to have your material milled to size before you bring it home. The hardwood lumber yard in L.A. where I bought the colorful hardwoods for this project also has a shop on site that was able to mill the lumber to size for me at a reasonable price.

After all the pieces are milled to perfect width and thickness by machine, you can cross cut them to length at home with a handsaw. I use a simple shop-made bench accessory called a bench hook. But you can also pick-up a plastic miter box for a few bucks at your local hardware store.

With all your pieces cut to size, you're ready to assemble them into a skateboard deck.

MARK THE BOARDS

Arrange the pieces on a flat work surface as they will be assembled. Take time to orient the wood grain just right. You want the show face to look nice, so hide any annoying knots or blemishes. You also want to do your best to ensure that the wood grain on each piece is oriented in the same direction. That becomes most important when you get to the shaping and finishing phase.

With the pieces aligned exactly as they will be glued, mark a large triangle on the show face that extends across each of the pieces of lumber. This triangle will allow you to easily realign the boards later if they happen to get out of order. It is also a quick and easy reference when you're under the gun during the glue-up.

KEEP UP WITH YOUR PARTS
Assemble all of the wood pieces without glue and mark a triangle at one end that spans each piece of wood. This way, if the parts get scattered you can easily realign them by lining up the triangle.

TAKE A DRY RUN WITH CLAMPS

Before you bust out the glue, do a practice assembly without glue to test out your process. When you're applying the glue, you have about nine minutes of "open time" to get all the surfaces covered in glue and assembled, so time your dry run and practice until you beat the clock.

Start by laying down a few scrap pieces of wood. These "cauls" raise the parts off the table and register one face of each board flat and aligned. Lay a matching set of cauls on top of the assembly in the same location as the bottom ones and secure them in place with clamps or rubber bands.

Now, apply clamps along the length of the deck. Start at one end and work your way to the other. Space the clamps about six to eight inches apart to apply even pressure across the entire edge joint.

SIMPLE CAULS KEEP IT FLAT
Straight hardwood cauls are clamped into place—one on top of the deck and one below—to keep the parts aligned during the glue-up.

TAKE A DRY RUN
Practice the all-important glue up with a dry run to get the hang of your setup and test the clamps.

LAY ON THE GLUE
Apply glue liberally but evenly to the joining edges of the wood strips with a small glue brush, available at hobby or hardware stores.

CHECK OUT YOUR WORK
Once your parts are assembled and clamped tightly, you can remove the cauls and flip it over.

GLUE IT UP

If your dry run worked and you completed it in less than nine minutes, it relieves a lot of the pressure when repeating it with glue.

Apply glue in an even coat across the entire glue surface of both sides of the joint. Many woods are thirsty and will drink up wet glue as soon as it's applied, so you want to make sure that every surface is wet before you join two boards. It's okay to let the glue sit on the surface for a few minutes while you're applying glue to the other pieces. In fact, this gives the glue some time to soak in. Fix any dry spots before the pieces go together.

With all joining edges covered in an even layer of glue, assemble them on the cauls and start adding clamps. The first clamp to go on should be at one end. Don't tighten it all the way just yet. Once you've got all the clamps on with mild pressure, then you can go back and tighten each clamp to its final pressure.

Don't over-tighten the clamps or you will squeeze out all of the glue and starve the joint, making it weak. Tighten the clamps just enough to close up the joint.

In 30 minutes, when the glue has turned from liquid to a rubbery goo, it's a good time to remove the glue that has overflowed from each joint. A razor blade works great for this. If the glue is too wet, it will make a big mess. If it's too dry, it's hard to remove. So make sure you wait long enough but not too long.

After a few hours when the glue has dried for good, remove the clamps and follow the same steps described in the previous project: Transfer your design from a paper template to the deck blank; cut it out to within 1⁄16 -in. to the line using a jigsaw outfitted with a 20 TPI blade; round-over the edge with a rasp and file; then drill the truck holes.

CLEAN UP THE SQUEEZE-OUT
A plain old razor blade does a good job of cleaning up the glue. For the best results, let the beads of glue dry for about 30 minutes so they pop right off instead of smearing glue everywhere.

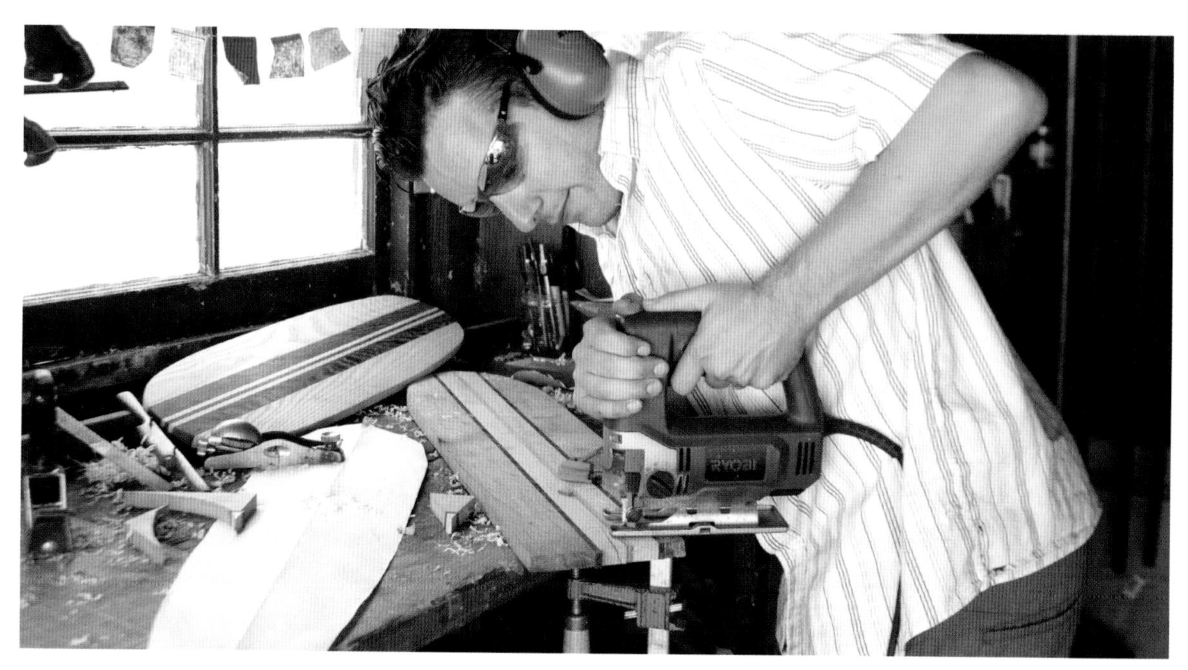

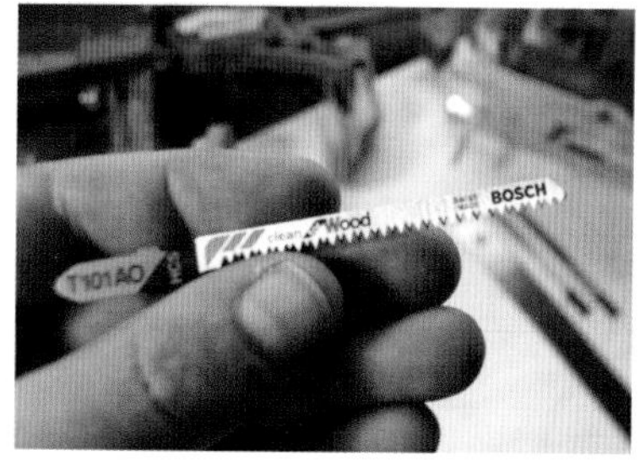

CUT THE BOARD TO SHAPE
Cut out the rough deck shape with a jigsaw and a fine-tooth blade. First use your template to mark out the line, then cut to within 1⁄16 of an inch.

TECHNIQUES FOR CUTTING AND SHAPING HARDWOOD

Now is a good time to introduce a few more woodworking tools and techniques that will make the job of cutting and shaping your deck a whole lot easier. Some are common tools you might already have laying around your garage. Others may be new to you and getting the hang of them will take a little practice.

If you've done a good job milling the lumber to a consistent thickness and you made sure all the boards aligned well during the glue up, you shouldn't have much work to do here. Usually, it won't take more than an hour to flatten and smooth the top and bottom surfaces to a final finish. (Conversely, if you haven't done a good job, and you have a lot of material to remove, you've got some work ahead.)

Have you ever petted a dog in the wrong direction, from tail to head? He hated it, right? That same sensation of going against the grain applies to cutting and shaping solid wood. When you're using cutting and shaping tools to shape a solid wood deck, don't "pet the dog" in the wrong direction. Use your tools in the same direction as the grain. This will help you avoid tearing out the surface of the wood.

To figure out which way you need to go, run your hand across the surface of the wood—the direction that feels more abrasive is usually against the grain. And beware of boards where the grain changes direction midway. If it does, cut and shape in both directions in different sections, always going with the grain.

SHORTCUT WITH POWER SANDERS

Hand sanding is a noble task, but if you don't have to do it, you might as well avoid it. An electric-powered random orbit sander will make quick work of an uneven surface. These specialized palm sanders work exactly as the name suggests: A pad of sandpaper moves at super-high speeds in a series of random orbital patterns. It sands the surface in such a way that it doesn't leave any scratch marks like hand sanding can. Just throw on a dust mask and some safety glasses, and keep the sander moving steadily across the entire surface.

When you've got a lot of material to remove, you may want to upgrade to a belt sander. Outfitted with 80-grit sandpaper, these aggressive cutting machines can remove a quarter inch of wood in less than 10 minutes—just watch out for the mushroom cloud of dust.

MAKE IT QUICK (above)
When it comes to speed and ease of use, nothing beats a random orbit palm sander for shaping a deck. Be sure you wear eye protection and a dust mask. Safety first!

REFINE THE SHAPE
A stationary belt sander is the ultimate tool for shaping a skate deck. Just be careful, it cuts fast. Keep the edge moving along the belt to prevent it from burning the wood or creating divots and notches.

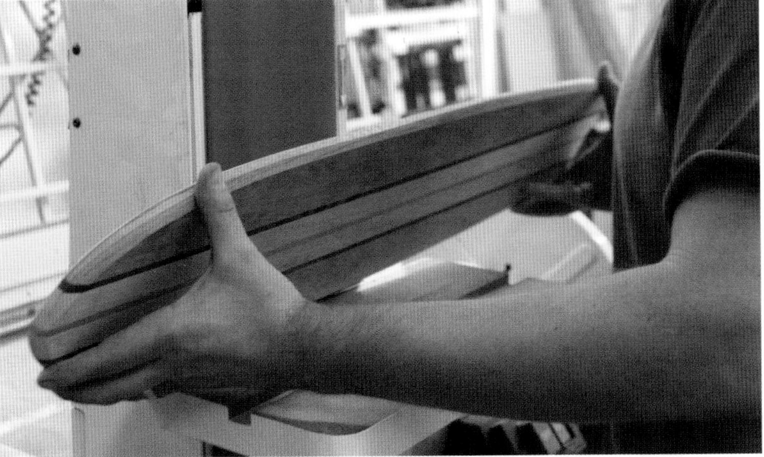

LET THE TOOL DO THE WORK
When rounding the edge on a stationary belt sander, sometimes you have to get a little creative. Make sure the work piece is always pressed down firmly against the fence.

REAL SKATEMAKERS USE HANDPLANES

If you take the time to learn how to use and maintain a handplane, you can remove material faster and with much less mess than sanding, and without the noise.

Believe it or not, before power sanders and even before electricity people shaped and cut wood using only hand-powered tools.

If you're up to the task, it's worth it to pick up some of these age-old skills, specifically how to use a handplane and a handsaw. Once you know how to use them, these simple hand tools can get the job done as quickly and accurately as a power tool, with the added benefit of no noise, lengthy setup, or excessive cleanup.

Block planes are a great place to start. They can be tricky to keep sharp and fit over the long haul. But if you take the time to learn how to use and maintain a handplane, you can remove material faster and with much less mess than sanding. Block planes are the most common type of plane and are great for rounding the edges of your deck. A block plane cuts long, thin shavings as you push it along a surface.

EASE THE EDGES WITH A PLANE
A block plane is a great tool for softening the edge of a hardwood deck. Once you get the hang of using one and keeping it sharp and tuned up, it's also a pleasure to use.

ACHIEVE A SMOOTH, CLEAN SHAVE
A utility blade serves as a poor-man's card scraper. Grip the blade tightly with your fingertips and tilt it forward as you scrape the surface of the wood.

AIM FOR SHAVINGS, NOT DUST
You know you're doing it right when you can produce a pile of shavings that look like pencil shavings. If you get dust, you're doing it wrong.

NO HAND TOOLS? IMPROVISE.

I don't expect you to have a tool chest full of hand tools, but there is one simple plane that you do probably have that's sharp and easy to use, even for a novice: a razor blade. It can replace your random-orbit sander to smooth and flatten surfaces for good.

Razor blades are available at any grocery store or pharmacy. They're scary sharp out of the package. They're cheap. They're disposable, which means you don't have to sharpen them. And they're easy to use.

Use the razor blade like an improvised card scraper, a traditional woodworking tool that's essentially a flat thin piece of metal with a "burr" honed onto the edge. When scraped across the surface of wood, a traditional card scraper cuts thin shavings to reveal a super smooth surface. But you can get the same results with a plain old razor blade. And you don't even have to tune it up first. Here's how:

Grip the blade with two hands, between your thumbs and your pointer and middle fingers. Rest the blade's edge against the surface of your material and tilt it forward slightly—about 80° from the surface.

Push the blade so that it scrapes across the surface and watch as it produces a thin shaving with each pass. Only cut on the push stroke. Lift it from the surface on the pull.

You know you're doing it right when you're left with a pile of shavings that look like they came out of a pencil sharpener. If you're left with a pile of dust, you're doing it wrong. Either tilt the blade farther forward or replace it because the blade has gone dull.

As always, rasps, files, and hand sanding are a good back-up plan if the razor blade hits a tricky spot. Only when working with hardwoods like oak and wenge is a lot of elbow grease required.

GRAB A COMBO TOOL
A 4-in-1 combination rasp and file is a great tool for softening and smoothing the edge you're your hardwood deck. It's also easy to use.

MAKE WAY FOR THE WHEELS
Start by roughing out the cove-shaped fenders using a rasp and file.

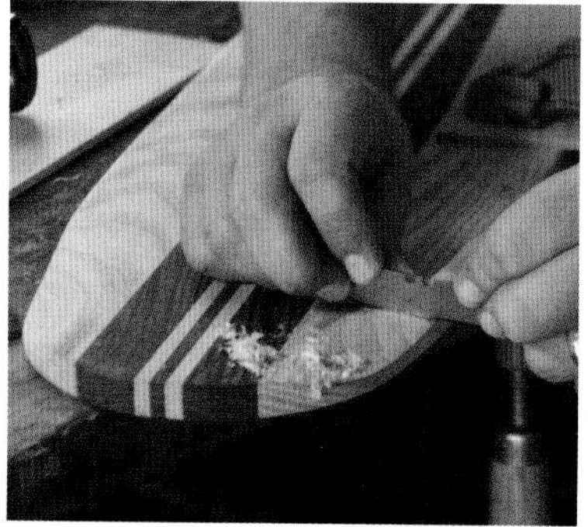

CLEAN UP THE SURFACE
Then use a razor blade scraper to smooth the surface and fair your curves.

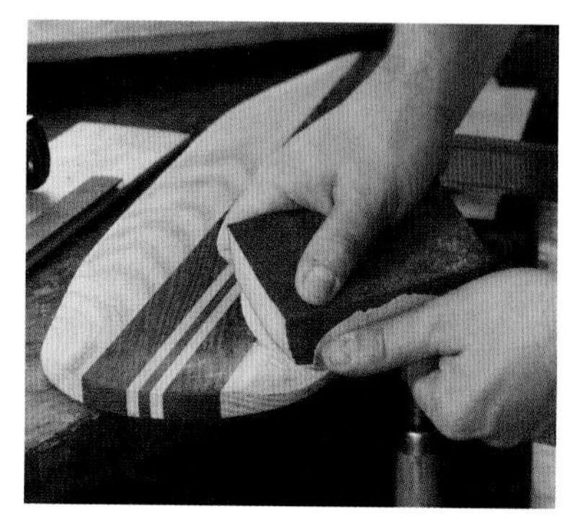

SMOOTH IT OUT
Then sand it to a finished surface using a flexible sanding block.

SHAPE FENDERS FOR MORE WHEEL CLEARANCE

When making a flat skateboard like this, it's important to design it so that the wheels don't come into contact with the deck when you lean into turns. If the wheel rubs the deck while riding, it will stop you in your tracks and send you flying through the air.

In the hackboard project, we avoided this by cutting fenders into the deck where the wheels line up. For a deck design like this one, the best approach is to carve cove-shaped fenders into the underside of the deck. This provides clearance for the wheels but doesn't interfere with the shape.

One way to shape these coves is with a 4-in-1 combination rasp and file. After marking the location with a pencil line for each cove on the deck, use the half-round rasp to chip away at the wood. Hold the tool at a near-flat angle as you cut.

Once the shape is mostly roughed out, switch to the file to smooth the cove. Finally, use a razor blade as scraper to bring the surface to a final finish.

If you have access to a community woodshop, look out for a specialty power called a spindle sander to accomplish this task. As the name suggests, it's a spindle wrapped in abrasive that spins at a high RPM and oscillates up and down to distribute the cut across the entire surface of the spindle.

It's an excellent tool for making the cove-shaped fenders. Choose a spindle with a large diameter, then press the deck against it until you have cut away the area within your marked lines.

SPINDLE SANDERS SPEED UP THE WORK
A spindle sander is a specialty tool. If you can find one, it's perfect for cutting the cove shaped fenders on the underside of some skate decks.

APPLY A SEALER COAT

The first coat of outdoor urethane finish goes on pretty heavy with a foam brush. The bare wood soaks up the finish like a sponge.

APPLY A SEALER COAT

When the surface is dry, sand it with 320-grit sandpaper to prep it for the next coat of finish. Finish the bottom surface to a final coat. About three to five applications is sufficient, sanding between each coat.

ADD GRIP IN THE FINISHING PROCESS

When you go to the effort of making a skateboard deck with decorative hardwoods and pinstripes, it's a shame to cover it with black grip tape. Instead you can create a clear grip on your deck during the finishing process with some basic hardware store supplies. It will preserve the natural wood's beauty while still providing enough grip to help footing when you ride.

There are a variety of materials you can try for a grip finish: Sand from a local beach works, but when you use enough of it to provide a good stick, it obscures the wood behind it in a dusty haze. The optimal product is finely crushed glass, sold as a specialty paint additive for texturing driveways and decks. Different brands of these additives use a variety of materials—not all are clear. An eco-friendly product sold at my local hardware store is made from crushed walnut shells.

DUST ON YOUR GRIP

On the final application of finish, sprinkle a coat of anti-skid grit to the wet surface evenly over the surface of the deck. It'll stick when the finish dries.

pro·file

NATURAL LOG SKATEBOARDS

WEBSITE:
www.naturallogskateboards.com

SK8MAKERS:
Eirik Nordgard and Thomas Brierton

WHERE:
San Diego, Calif.

FEATURED DECK:
Vintage Roots Mini 24"

Natural Log Skateboards started as a hobby for co-owners and friends Eirik Nordgard and Thomas Brierton. But it didn't take long for the two to get bitten by the skatemaker bug and turn their hobby into a thriving internet business run out of a roomy garage workshop in their hometown of San Diego.

With a collection of tools, jigs, and state-of-the-art finishing equipment, the two churn out a collection of high-quality handmade decks of different shapes and sizes that share one important trait: a focus on craftsmanship and sustainable materials.

Their trademark deck, the Vintage Roots, is a great example of the type of work they produce. Each deck is pressed with a top and bottom layer of reclaimed barn wood, hand-picked and resawn into thin veneers on the bandsaw. The barnwood veneers are laminated to a bamboo core in a two-part press rigged up in their shop. The veneers and bamboo core are glued up with an epoxy adhesive made mostly from tree sap, called Entropy Super Sap Resin, completing the environmentally-friendly package.

The duo doesn't have plans any time soon to take their operation large scale. For now, they're happy getting by building one skateboard at a time. "I think we represent a new type of business where you can work out of the garage, but still reach the masses online," Nordgard says.

SHAPING AT THE BANDSAWN
Eirik Nordgard, co-owner of Natural Log Skateboards, rough cuts a glued-up skateboard blank on the bandsaw in his San Diego, Calif., garage workshop.

ALL PHOTOS COURTESY OF NATURAL LOG SKATEBOARDS.

TEMPLATES GUARANTEE UNIFORMITY
Thomas Brierton, co-owner of Natural Log Skateboards, cuts the deck shape on a router table with a bearing-guided router template.

MAKING SAWDUST (above)
Eirik Nordgard, observing proper safety precautions, is hard at work sanding one of the company's trademark skateboard decks.

FINISHING TOUCHES
Thomas Brierton laying out and marking a near-complete deck for the final finishing process.

SPRAY-ON TAN
The two-man team complete their decks with a spray-on finish, producing a super high-quality sheen to the final product.

THE FINISHED DECK
The Vintage Roots cruiser deck from Natural Log Skateboards is laminated from recycled vintage oak lumber.

ALL PHOTOS COURTESY OF NATURAL LOG SKATEBOARDS.

CHAPTER 5

HOW TO BUILD A BERGERBOARD LONGBOARD

The first deck I ever built from scratch looked a lot like the classic pinstripe longboard in this chapter. In fact, I made so many of them in my college woodshop that they affectionately became known as Bergerboards.

The design is somewhat primitive compared to a modern skateboard or longboard deck since it's mostly flat. But one significant addition to the design makes this a more complex build than the flat decks in previous chapters: a bent kicktail. The bend is accomplished using a technique called bent lamination, in which multiple layers of wood are glued together in a stack while compressed into a bend under heavy clamping pressure. When the glue dries, voilà. The lamination holds its shape.

In addition to bending wood, this project involves another advanced woodworking technique used to create colorful pinstripes on the top and bottom of the deck. While some of these processes might seem like a stretch if you have modest woodworking experience, a few tips and tricks make it easy to complete with basic tools.

CARRY A BIG STICK
This classic longboard offers a comfortable, relaxing ride for all ages and sizes. A gentle kicktail adds extra leverage for steering this big ship down the boardwalk or the sidewalk.

the goods

TOOLS
Jigsaw or bandsaw, trim router, sander (electric or hand-powered), drill-driver with ¼-in. drill-and-countersink bit.

MATERIALS
⅛-thick plywood, ⅛-in-thick hardwood, PVA wood glue, polyurethane wood finish.

EQUIPMENT
Shopmade clamping press, air compressor and pneumatic brad nailer (or hammer and brads), at least 8 bar clamps, safety glasses, dust mask.

SETUP
Trucks and wheels will vary in size depending on the size and shape; bearings; risers; grip tape or silicon grip.

the bergerboard

Made from multiple layers of thinly sawn wood, a Bergerboard is an easy introduction to laminating veneers and bending wood. Not to mention, it makes for a sweet ride.

LENGTH:
41 in.

WIDTH:
8 ¾ in.

WHEEL SPAN:
28 in.

MATERIALS:
Hardwood (bubinga, maple), ⅛-in. Baltic birch plywood

TRUCKS:
Independent 169

RISERS:
½-in. wedge risers

BEARINGS:
Bones REDS

WHEELS:
76 mm urethane wheels

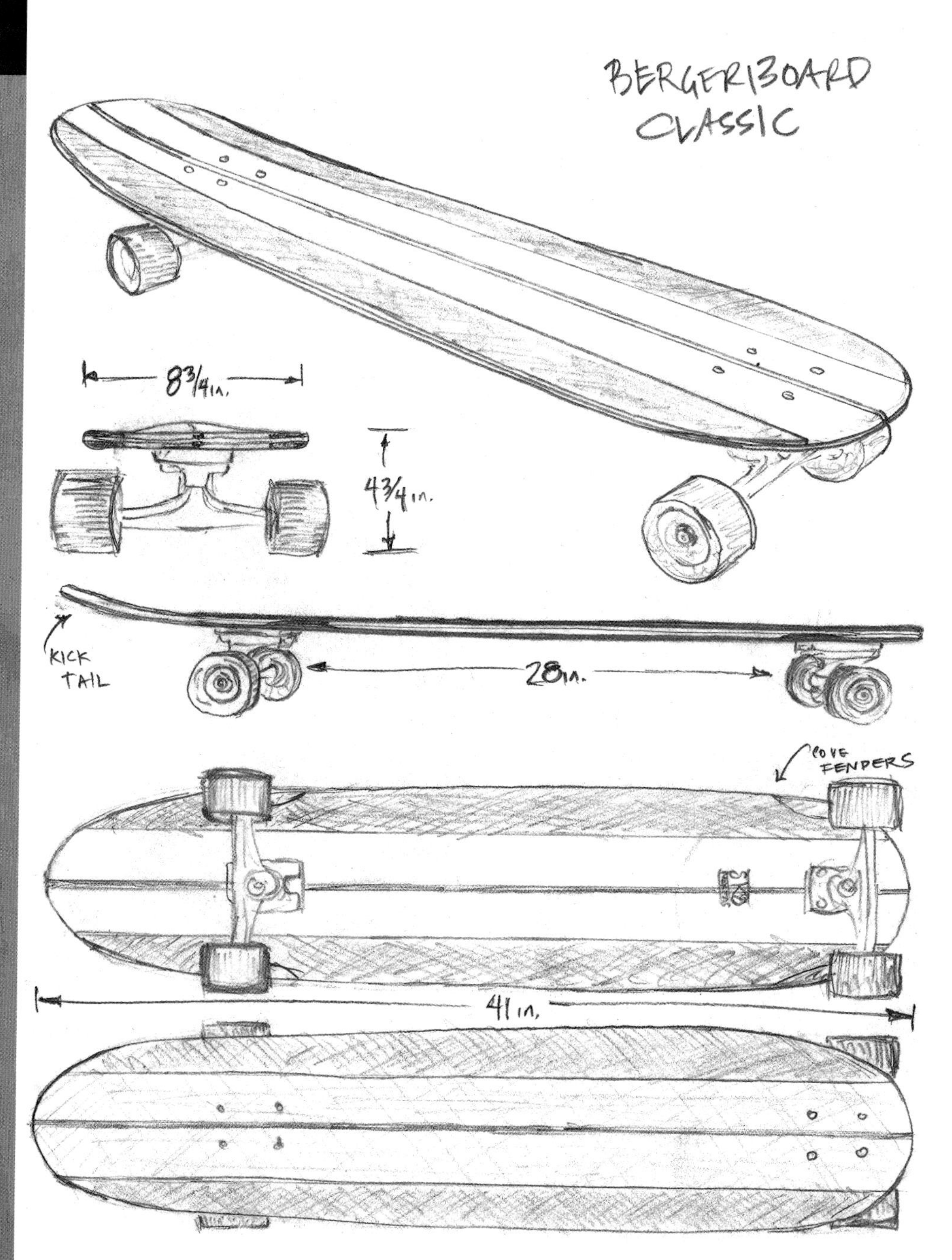

TAKING STOCK OF THE PLIES
To create a kicktail in this deck, four thin layers of material are assembled in a clamping press. The top and bottom layers are hardwood. The center consists of two sheets of ⅛-in.-thick Baltic birch plywood.

PRESS YOUR OWN PLYWOOD FROM COLORFUL HARDWOODS

To build this deck, you are essentially making your own plywood from four layers of thin wood. The top and bottom layers are composed of five strips of hardwood—to parts maple, three parts Bubinga—cut ⅛-in. thick. Sandwiched in between the hardwood layers are two sheets of ⅛-in. thick Baltic birch plywood. The thin layers are flexible enough to bend in the clamping press, but when stacked and glued together they create a solid deck just over ½ in. thick.

The first step in preparing the lumber for this build is to cut the hardwood pieces to size. These parts are cut to size using a tablesaw for ripping and crosscutting each piece to final dimensions and a jointer and planer to flatten and square up the the stock.

If you have the tools and skills to pull that off, great. If you don't, you have two options. Substitute the top and bottom layers with ⅛-in. Baltic birch plywood or have a hardwood dealer cut the pieces to size for you. The parts for this deck came milled to size from my favorite Los Angeles lumberyard, House of Hardwoods. I picked out the most prime rough lumber from their stock and paid for it to be cut to finished dimension.

The key to dimensioning your lumber is that all four layers of the deck measure the same width and length. When you cut the pieces to create the pinstripe pattern on the top and bottom of the deck, you have to do the math to ensure that when all the hardwood parts are lined up edge to edge, they are as wide as the plywood layers.

A SIMPLE WAY TO BEND
A block of wood at one end of the press elevates the lamination to create a bend for the kicktail. An extra clamping block at the end of the deck complete the glue-up.

1 POSITION THE PARTS
To assemble the torsion box, apply glue to the wood strips and arrange them on the bottom skin.

BUILD A SHOP-MADE CLAMPING PRESS

Before you get started building the longboard deck, you first need to build a clamping press to press all four layers of wood. The design for this press is called a torsion box. The strong, lightweight design consists of three main elements: A top skin, a bottom skin, and a honeycomb of wood "ribs" in between. When assembled, the elements work together to create a virtually unbendable structure that is super strong and sturdy. It offers the same clamping strength as a solid block of wood, but it's much lighter and can be assembled with inexpensive materials and scrap wood.

The base of the press measures 10 in. wide by 48 in. long. It has a thin block attached to one edge, which acts as a fence to align all of the wood during glue up. It also has a block at one end that is used to create the bend. Two feet on the underside of the base elevate it above the workbench so you can fit your clamps underneath during assembly. The top of the clamping press should measure about as wide as your finished deck. It's also shorter than the base to allow the laminated layers of wood to bend.

Assembling the torsion box parts for the top and bottom of the press follow the same process. First, lay down the bottom plywood skin. Then assemble the internal honeycomb piece by piece. Apply glue to each piece as you go, then tack it in place with a pneumatic nailer (or hammer and brad) to keep them steady while the glue dries. There's no real rhyme or reason to the layout of the honeycomb. The important thing is that each piece is perfectly equal in thickness so that when you lay the top skin down it is flush and level across the entire surface.

Your clamping press is almost complete. Add the wedge block at one end with a spot of glue. Lastly, attach a pair of feet to keep the press elevated off your workbench so that the clamps can fit underneath.

2 SECURE THEM IN PLACE
Attach the strips with a pneumatic nailer to hold each part tightly in place while the glue dries. Once assembled, the solid, lightweight base is bomb-proof.

3 CLOSE UP THE BOX

Apply glue to the top edge and attach the top skin to the torsion box with a few nails. If you don't have a pneumatic nailer, a few small brads and a hammer work as well.

4 ADD EXTRA STRENGTH

The clamping press is almost ready to use. Attach a few more strips on the top of the clamping block to add more strength. This top block is shorter than the base to create the bend for the kicktail. Notice that the width of the top is based off of the dry-fit deck.

5 SEAL IT UP

Cover the clamping press in clear packing tape to make glue squeezeout easier to remove from the jig and to prevent the laminations from sticking to the jig.

1 START WITH THE CORE
Roll an even layer of glue onto the top face of the plywood core. Then flip the core and apply glue to the opposite face.

2 LAY THE LAYERS IN PLACE
Roll a thin even layer of glue on the mating pieces to ensure a good glue bond between the two surfaces.

3 AIM FOR TIGHT SEAMS
With a few clamps in place to apply light vertical pressure, close any gaps between the wood strips on the top and bottom by setting clamps across the board's width.

pro tip

DETERMINE THE POSITION OF THE TRUCK AND WHEELS

Sometimes you have to feel out the best position for the trucks and wheels. I like to do this after the deck is glued up but before I cut out the shape and drill the truck holes. Too far apart, and the deck is hard to steer. Too close, and it can become out of balance. To find just the right position, I place short blocks underneath the deck and stand on it, repositioning the blocks until it feels just right. The goal is to locate the trucks far enough apart to accomodate your open stance, but not so far apart as that the board has too much flex in the center.

PRESS YOUR DECK

With your material milled and your press assembled, it's time to glue up your deck. The most important thing in this step of the process is to ensure that the hardwood strips that make up the pinstripes are perfectly straight, with square edges and even thickness. If these parts don't have good edges, there will be gaps in the glue line.

Begin by stacking and arranging all of the parts in order, and then place the stack on the bottom of the clamping press with the tail-end resting on top of the wood block. If you haven't covered your press in packing tape, lay down a sheet of wax paper to prevent the parts from becoming glued to the press. Apply glue liberally to all joining surfaces as quickly as you can. Make sure there's glue on the edges of the hardwood pin stripes to ensure a clean glue line on the top and bottom surfaces. When all of the parts are glued and assembled, wrap the stack with masking tape to hold the parts in place while you align it on the press. Finally, lay a sheet of wax paper on top.

Now start clamping. It takes at least eight clamps to press the deck. I also use some mini-clamps and cauls to keep the tail end joined tightly while the glue dries. After about eight hours, remove the clamps to reveal your freshly pressed longboard blank.

KEEP IT CLEAN

To keep dust to a minimum, rely on an inexpensive razor blade as your primary surfacing tool. Use it as a scraper to smooth the top and bottom of your deck.

SHAPE YOUR DECK WITH HAND AND POWER TOOLS

If you've decided to take on this longboard project then you're probably not afraid of woodworking tools. You might even have a few of your own, or at least access to a woodshop with power tools and woodworking machines. That's good, because using power tools will help you complete this deck a lot more quickly than using handtools alone. For starters, you'll save time and get a cleaner edge if you shape the deck using a bandsaw instead of a jigsaw.

The more consistent in thickness your materials were from the beginning, the less work you'll have finishing the top and bottom surfaces of your deck. Depending on your own preferences, you could go with a belt sander or a random orbit sander to surface both sides of the deck blank—either is an fine choice. If you don't have power sanders, stick with the method described in the vintage pinstripe chapter—use a disposable razor blade to scrape the surface smooth and even.

If you're upgrading to a bandsaw, then you might as well also upgrade to a laminate trimmer to round the edge. This mini router was originally designed for trimming the edges of delicate laminate countertops, but does an equally good job trimming skateboard edges. I use a ⅛-in. round-over bit with a bottom-mounted bearing guide. Set the bit height so that the bearing runs along the center of the deck, then trim all the way around, working from left to right.

ROUNDOVER BY MACHINE

Tired of shaping the edge of your skateboard decks with handtools? Upgrade to a trim router with a bearing-guided ⅛-in. roundover bit. Clamp down your work and go.

ROUT IT OUT

Run your laminate trimmer all the way around the top and bottom edges of the deck. As you work your way around the deck, reset the clamps so they stay out of your way.

KEEP IT GRITTY
Rather than cover up the decorative veneers on the top with traditional grip tape, mix silicon grit into your finish. It dries clear doesn't detract from the shine.

FINISHING TOUCHES

Finally, drill the holes for the trucks and finish them off with a countersink. Once the holes are drilled, sand the board to a final finish. For this board, I hand sand through 320 grit.

Similar to the vintage pinstripe deck, I don't cover the top surface with grip tape. If you've gone through all this effort to make a colorful pinstripe deck you don't want to hide it. Instead, mix silicon grit into your finishing process for a clear grip coat.

Similar to the vintage pinstripe deck, I didn't cover the top surface of this one with grip tape. I've gone through all this effort to make a colorful pinstripe deck and I don't want to hide it behind a sheet of black.

This time, I mixed the silicon grit in with the clear urethane finish and painted it on with a brush. I thinned down the urethane and silicon grit mixture with a tablespoon or so of mineral spirits to help thin the finish and make it easier to paint on.

pro·file

LOYAL DEAN SKATEBOARDS

SK8MAKER:
Dino Pierone

WHAT:
Loyal Dean Skateboards

WHERE:
Los Angeles, Calif.

WEBSITE:
www.loyaldean.com

It turns out that a woodshop set up to build high-end custom doors and windows also makes a great skateboard factory on the side. If you don't believe me, then take a look at Dino Pierone and his South Los Angeles shop RJ Doors, home to the custom skateboard brand, Loyal Dean.

The busy shop is massive on every scale, from the type of work being produced (doors that are three times the size of the humans building them) to the equipment and machinery used to produce these things. But it's this large-scale setup that enables the shop to turn out some of the most interesting woodwork to ever be featured on a skateboard deck.

Loyal Dean's speciality is the decorative geometric designs made from wood featured on the top and bottom layers of each deck. Scraps and strips of colorful hardwoods are laminated into blocks in a way that produces complex designs that trick the eye. Loyal Dean's lamination process is so specialized that it can really only be accomplished using the large-scale machines that are required to assemble massive windows and doors.

While Loyal Dean started off as a hobby, it's turning into a lucrative business. With each new batch of decks produced, Dino and his crew are trying new ways to make the process more efficient and scalable while still maintaining their unique spin on the art and design of skateboard making.

READY FOR DELIVERY
A complete Loyal Dean skateboard deck sits on the rack at the company's South Los Angeles woodshop awaiting delivery to a retail destination.

A FINISHED DECK
The top surface of the latest batch of Loyal Dean skateboards features a colorful assortment of exotic veneeers. It's topped with protective finish and a see-through layer of sandy grit that does the job of griptape without obscuring the design.

A DOUBLE-DUTY SHOP
Loyal Dean co-founder Dino Pierone gives a tour of the shop, which is primarily used to create massive doors and windows for high-end customers in Los Angeles and Orange County.

THINK BIG
One of the many massive tools used to create a Loyal Dean skateboard is this industrial resaw machine. Similar to a bandsaw, it uses a continuous blade to cut thin sheets of wood from a large block. A conveyer belt helps move the wood block through the blade while the wheels on top feed it through and keep the material pressed flat against the table.

ADD A LITTLE COLOR
The secret sauce revealed! This stack of laminated woods represnets just step one in the complex process of creating a Loyal Dean skateboard deck.

SKATERS NEEDED
Loyal Dean skateboard decks lie in wait at the company's South Los Angeles woodshop.

CHAPTER 6

HOW TO BUILD A SKATE DECK FROM A KIT

It's hard to write a book about making DIY skateboard decks without devoting a chunk of space to the Roarockit method, an innovative approach to building a professional-quality skateboard deck with simple tools and techniques that an ambitious kid can build at the kitchen table (with a little help from Dad, of course).

Sounds crazy, right?

Well, it's not, and I enlisted my kids to prove it using one of Roarockit's pre-shaped kits. Roarockit kits are available in the shape of a street deck, a pin-tail longboard, or a mini cruiser based on the popular Penny boards and inspired by the 1970s banana boards. When you buy one of these kits, a lot of the hard work has been done for you. The maple veneers come cut to shape; the truck holes are pre-drilled on the bottom veneer; and each kit comes with a shaped foam mold and the hand-operated vacuum bag system that makes it all possible. Follow the one-page instruction manual and you can put together a Roarockit deck in a weekend.

There's even more upside to this method: It's the fastest, most accurate, and most durable approach to garage-shop deck building. And once you understand the process, the design possibilities are limitless.

A FAMILY PROJECT
Built from a Roarockit kit, this seven-layer deck is not only easy to put together, it's also bulletproof. Kits are available in a variety of styles.

the goods

TOOLS
4-in-1 combination rasp/file, Stanley Surform, drill-driver with ¼-in drill bit, countersink bit, hand sanding block.

MATERIALS
7 layers 1⁄16-in. maple veneer (five long-grain, two cross grain, all in the kit), PVA wood glue, polyurethane wood finish.

EQUIPMENT
Dust mask, safety glasses, paint roller. From the kit: Thin Air Press Vacuum Bag, hand pump, shaped foam mold.

SETUP
Trucks and wheels (size may vary depending on the size and shape of your finished deck), bearings, risers, grip tape.

roarockit street deck

Just because a kid can build it with adult supervision, doesn't mean the Roarockit kit isn't a legit street deck. Follow the directions carefully and you'll end up with a top-quality, handcrafted skateboard that rivals those for sale at your local skateshop.

LENGTH:
31 in.

WIDTH:
7 ⅞ in.

WHEEL SPAN:
14 in.

MATERIALS:
Maple veneer
(Seven 1⁄16-in.-thick layers)

TRUCKS:
Independent 129

RISERS:
⅛-in. plastic risers

BEARINGS:
Bones REDS

WHEELS:
52 mm street

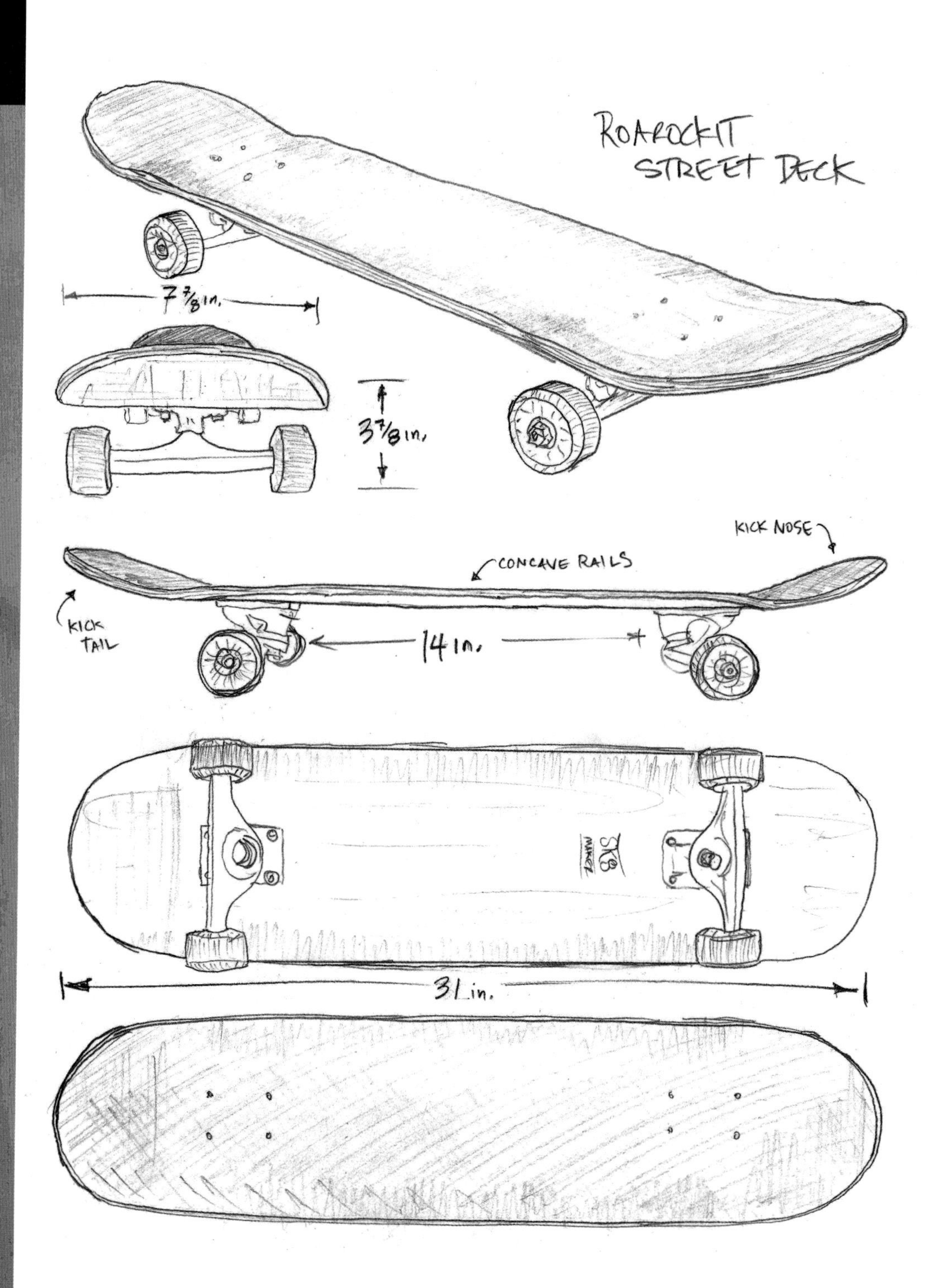

ANATOMY OF A 7-PLY DECK

The Roarockit kit produces a strong and stable skateboard deck, just like the commercial decks available at your local skateshop, by laminating seven layers of 1⁄16 -in.-thick maple veneer to create a plywood deck with complex curves and bends.

Historically, skateboard manufacturers have relied on industrial-grade hydraulic presses to laminate the veneer into decks, but that kind of setup is too expensive for the garage-shop skatemaker. Roarockit has reduced the process to one that requires only simple accessories and handtools.

The technique borrows from the decades-old method of vacuum pressing, which was originally applied to woodworking around World War II for making wooden aircraft parts. In the late 1980s, furniture makers adopted the process to produce complex furniture parts like curved doors and drawer fronts, and to adhere decorative veneers to the surface of a tabletop.

The vacuum press system works like this: Thin sheets of wood veneer are coated in glue and stacked on a mold shaped to the inverse of your finished product. The mold and veneers are then placed inside an airtight bag made of thick plastic. All of the air inside the bag is extracted through a valve with a vacuum pump, forcing the veneers to bend to the shape of the mold. When the glue dries, the lamination is removed from the bag and, violà, it holds its shape.

Where Roarockit has innovated this process is in the method used to extract the air from the bag. Vacuum press systems traditionally relied on an expensive electric-powered vacuum pump to draw the air out. Instead, Roarockit uses a simple hand-powered pump originally designed to pull the air out of wine bottles. The kit also innovates on the mold, using high-density foam instead of traditional steel or cement molds.

HAND-POWERED VACUUM PRESS Ted Hunter and his wife, Norah Jackson hold a patent on the Roarockit tools and process. The technique it's based on—bending wood to a mold in a thick plastic bag with a vacuum press—was originally used to create airplane parts. Ted improved on the method using foam and an inexpensive handpump originally designed to re-seal wine bottles.

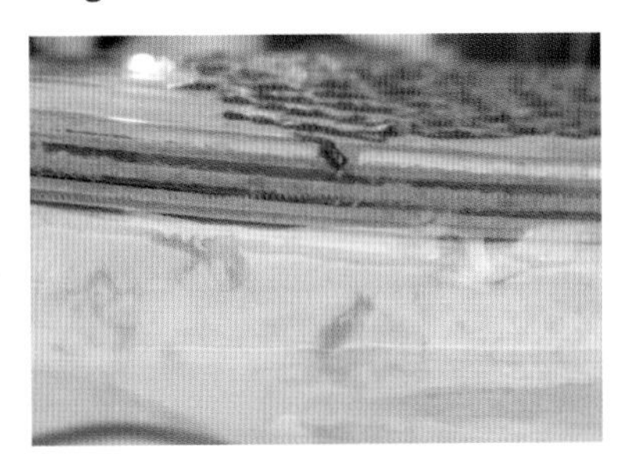

TAKE A DRY RUN

It's a good idea to practice the vacuum press process without glue before you commit to a real glue-up. This will help you get your bearings and make sure all your equipment is set up and easily in reach.

Roarockit recommends pressing the deck in three stages. Why? Well: You have to get the glue on, put the layers bag the deck, align the veneers perfectly on the mold, and pump out all the air in seven minutes flat (before the glue sets). Attempting all that with seven layers of veneer is challenging. Doing it with three or four layers of veneer gives you a much greater chance of getting it right.

SURVEY THE PARTS
Before the glue-up, the team examines all of the parts and materials that come with the Roarockit kit: Glue? Check. Veneers? Check. Foam mold? Check. Veneer bag, netting, and pump? Check.

Start by organizing the veneers in the order that they will be assembled. The five long-grain veneers are used for the two layers on top (No. 1, No. 2), two layers on the bottom (No. 6 and No. 7), and one layer in the center (No. 4). Layers No. 3 and No. 5 run cross grain.

Next, run through the process without glue, stacking the veneers on the mold, placing them in the bag, setting the netting in place (it allows the air a path out of the bag), sealing the bag, and pumping out the air.

If you don't completely seal the end of the bag, air will leak and prevent the veneer layers from forming to the mold. The Roarockit kit comes with a thick gooey tape to seal the end of the bag. When fully sealed, the tape will appear shiny on both sides where it adheres to the bag. Air leaks usually appear as light-gray colored spots in the goo.

PRACTICE MAKES PERFECT
It's critical that you have all of the parts on hand and know what you're doing when the glue goes on. The easiest way to make sure everything goes smoothly is to do a dry run before adding glue to the mix.

PUMP IT UP!
The hand-held vacuum pump draws air from the vacuum bag. While one person pumps, the other keeps the veneer in place and prevents the plastic from slipping between the deck and the foam mold.

Vacuum veneering is a well-tested method used for buiding everything from chairs to airplane components. The hand pump used here for extracting air serves the same purpose as the large electric pumps used for industrial applications.

pro tip

DON'T BOTHER WITH CLEAN-UP

Once you've charged your roller with glue, store it in a sealed plastic bag. The glue will stay wet for as long as the bag is sealed and you'll be able to reuse your roller over and over again.

THE GLUE-UP

When you're able to complete a dry run in under seven minutes flat, it's time to bust out the glue and do it again. This time for real. If you're unsure of your ability to beat the clock, keep practicing without glue until you're confident in the process.

The key to a high-quality lamination is in how you apply the glue: too much and you're likely to fumble the process; not enough glue and you'll starve the joint, increasing your chances of the board delaminating later on. Your goal is to be like Goldilocks and get it just right.

For an even, quick glue application, use a 3-in. wide paint roller. Each Roarockit kit comes with a glue roller and a measuring cup that helps you apply the right amount of glue on each layer.

Start by pouring 2½ cupfuls of glue on the inside face of layer No. 7. On this first application, the glue will soak into the roller, so you won't need as much glue on subsequent layers.

If you see a big shiny pool of glue form on the veneer, that's a problem; you're using too much. All that extra glue will squeeze out the sides like an

The key to a strong skateboard deck is the criss-cross layers of veneer. The inner sheets of the deck are oriented with the grain facing in alternating directions, weaving the wood fibers into a super stable deck that can take a real beating.

POUR IT ON
Arrange the layers of maple veneer and pour out a small, manageable amount of glue. It's easier to add a little more glue if needed than it is to remove glue.

ROLL IT OUT
Use the included roller to apply the glue. If you see shiny pools of glue, you've applied too much; dull spots mean you haven't applied enough. Find a helper to hold down the veneer stack and keep it aligned as you apply glue to the sheet.

overflowing waffle maker and create a mess of your kit. It could also create air bubbles in the deck during the drying process that could ruin a glue-up. Because the glue dries faster at the edges than in the center of the deck, a pool of glue in the center will cause the maple veneers to expand in the only direction they can go: up.

You also don't want to use too little glue, and starve the joint. The instruction manual doesn't require it, but I like to apply a thin layer of glue to the adjoining face of veneer (layer No. 6) at the same time to prime the surface. This helps prevent the glue from soaking into the wood before it has time to adhere to the joining piece. It also preps the wood by raising the grain, which makes them stick together like Velcro.

When you've finished applying glue to each layer, press the pieces together and hold them in place while you continue applying glue to the next veneer faces. It helps to have a least one person pitching in to hold the veneers steady and aligned while awaiting the next layer.

PRESS THE DECK

With glue applied to the first three layers of veneer, stack them on the foam mold and insert the assembly into the vacuum bag. Then lay the supplied breather netting on the top veneer so that it is directly underneath the air valve. This will help you pull the air from all corners of the bag. Without it, the bag can seal prematurely and leave air trapped inside pockets of the bag.

Finally, seal the bag with the gooey tape. This step is the most crucial step in the process because it prevents air from getting into the bag when you use the hand pump as a vacuum. Try to keep the tape clean and in decent shape—it can be reused on later projects.

The second most crucial step of the glue-up is to make sure the veneers stay aligned and flush with each other and with the foam mold. If you don't align the parts properly on the mold, the pre-drilled truck holes on the bottom veneer layer won't line up in parallel with the edge of the deck, and you may end up with a narrower board than you expected.

With the bag sealed, quickly begin pulling out the air with the hand-held pump. Again, it helps to have a few extra hands around to improve your results. As the air is extracted, your helpers should focus on preventing the bag from creeping between the foam mold and the veneer layers. Pull the edges of the bag away from the mold periodically to prevent it from interfering with the glue-up. Your helper can also press down on each end of the deck to help the veneers bend to the shape of the kick nose and tail.

Seven minutes after your first glue roll, you should have everything in the bag and the air extracted. If you don't, HURRY UP!

Now, take a few minutes to relax and assess your glue-up. Are all the veneers aligned? Are there any gaps in the veneers? Has the bag crept under the deck? Is the bag leaking air? If anything needs adjustment, quickly let a little air in to release the pressure and make the fix. Then pump it again. For the next two hours, check the bag periodically to make sure that the seal doesn't break. If you're good, leave the veneers in the bag for at least eight hours while the glue dries.

The Roarockit instructions recommend that you complete the glue up in three sessions. That means you'll need to repeat the above process two more times, adding a few more layers of veneer with each glue-up.

If you get really good at it, or you have enough helpers on hand, you can actually glue up all seven layers at once. The vacuum bag is strong enough to bend all seven layers at once. But can you glue each piece adequately, keep them aligned, and bag and pump in under seven minutes? It's better to glue up in a few different rounds—especially if this is your first time.

SEAL IT UP
Sealing the bag is the most important step in the vacuum press process. It's also a good idea to have a partner around to hold the veneers steady while sealing the bag.

PUMP IT OUT!
The hand-held vacuum pump draws air from the valve on the vacuum bag. While one person is removing the air, the other two should be keeping the veneers steady and preventing the plastic from slipping between the wood deck and the foam mold.

ADD ANOTHER LAYER

After eight hours, remove the lamination and foam mold from the vacuum bag and start the second round. Apply glue to the exposed surface of the lamination and add the next three layers of veneer.

pro tip

TROUBLESHOOTING THE GLUE-UP

If you end up with bubbles or ripples in your lamination, don't worry. They can be fixed. Slice open the area with a utility knife, inject glue into the space, and then press it back together with a clamp or by putting it back in the vacuum bag and evacuating the air. The same is true if the edges of your deck don't completely adhere. There's no shame in patching up your board; it will help make the deck stronger so it lasts longer.

DO IT AGAIN

Pump the air from the bag a second time, again with some helpers to keep the plastic from creeping between the mold and the deck.

PATIENCE YOUNG SK8MAKER

The deck must remain in the bag for at least eight hours for the glue to set and dry. And no, watching it doesn't help glue dry.

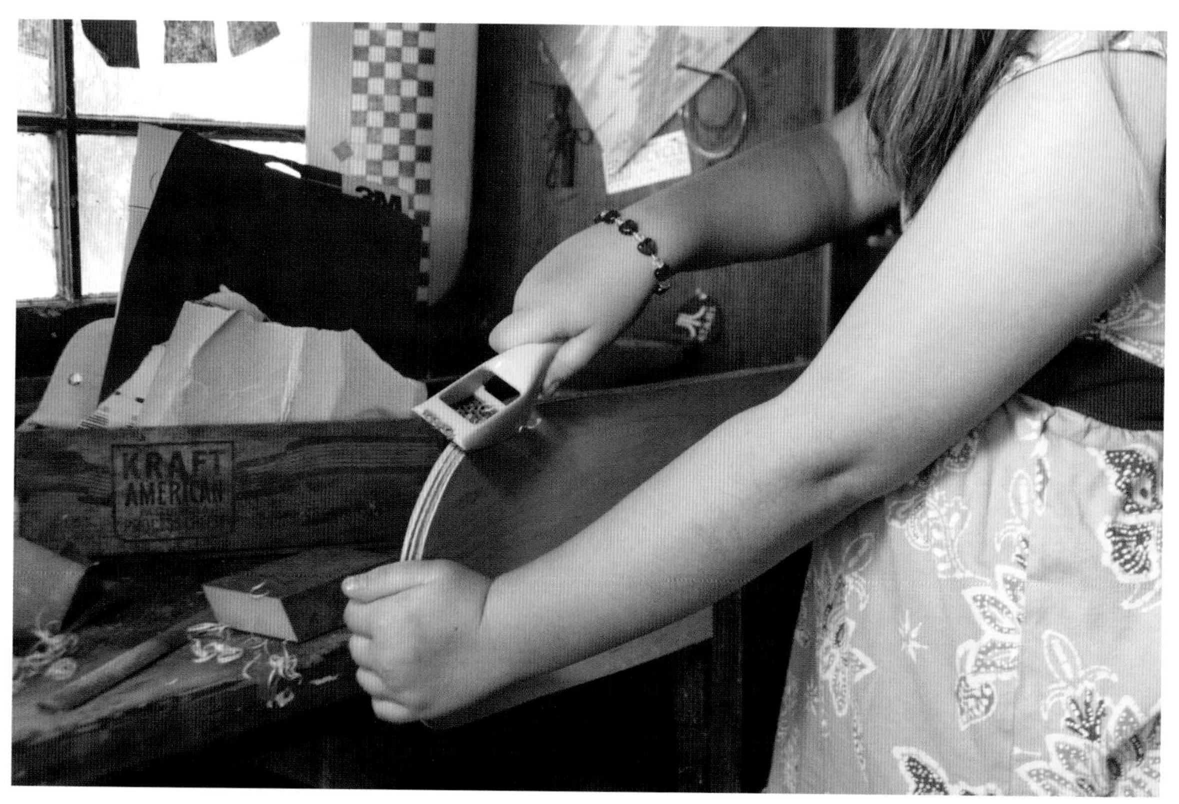

SMOOTH THE EDGES

Roarockit includes a Stanlely Surform in each kit to help you shape the edge of the deck. It works like a cheese grater, slicing away excess material.

SHAPE THE DECK AND DRILL THE HOLES

After all seven layers of veneer have been assembled and the glue is dry, it's time to shape your deck and drill the truck holes. The Roarockit kit arrives with most of the hard work already done for you.

Because the veneers come pre-cut (and hopefully you've done a nice job aligning the veneers during assembly), you only have a minimal amount of shaping to do. Roarockit supplies a Stanley Surform handtool with each kit to accomplish this task. Similar to a rasp, the Surform cuts away at the wood like a cheese grater.

First, create a perfectly flat, square edge all the way around the perimeter of the deck. Your goal is to establish the final deck shape and get all the edges flush, flat, and even.

When you've completed that square edge, soften the sharp corners to create a half-round edge. Start with the SurForm tool, cutting a 45° bevel on the top and bottom edges of the deck, then round the hard edges and finish up with a sanding block or electric sander.

FINE TUNE THE EDGES
Once the basic shape is roughed out, fair the curves and refine the shape uising using rasps or a flat-blade Surform.

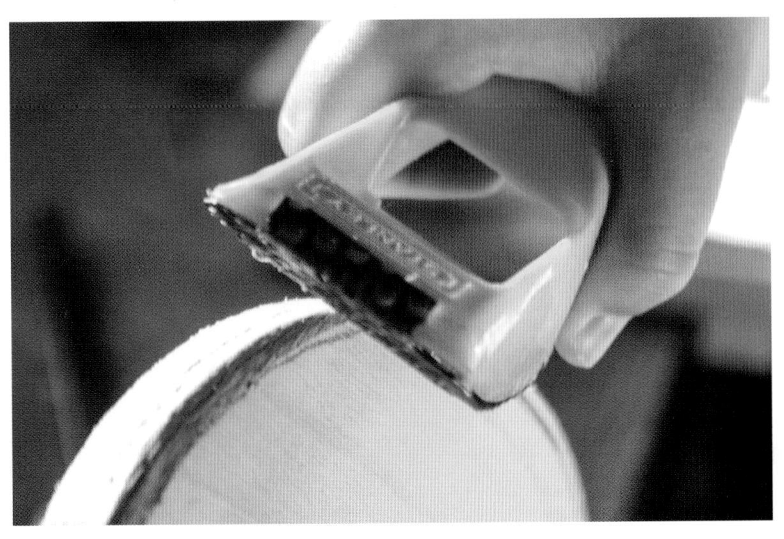

EASE THE EDGES
Once the perimeter of the deck is shaped to your template and the edge is 90° to the surface, use the curved blade Surform tool included in the kit to round the edge.

pro tip

BELT SAND BY HAND

To save time and ease the labor, rip a 100-grit sanding belt into strips and use one like a polishing strap to round-over the edge. Secure your deck to a workbench or table with a clamp or vice.

As it turns out, a skateboard deck is the perfect DIY project for teaching kids how to build things from scatch, by hand.

Lastly, drill the truck holes from the bottom of the board up. Since the kit comes with one veneer layer pre-drilled, this is an easy task. Just use those holes to guide your drill bit. Make sure the deck has a backer board where the bit will exit the cut to prevent tearout.

THE FINISH LINE

The last step before your deck is complete is to apply a clear coat on all sides to seal the wood. If you don't have time to apply a finish immediately after shaping, put the deck and mold back in the vacuum bag and store it with the air compressed until you are ready. If you don't clear coat soon after removing the lamination from the bag, it may dry out too quickly and cause the deck to warp, bend, or twist.

A LITTLE ELBOW GREASE
The ladies take a break from their street decks for some finish sanding on a pair of Roarockit Mini skateboards.

DRILL FOR THE TRUCKS
Roarockit kits come with the truck holes drilled on the bottom layer. Use those marks to guide your drill bit and be sure to place a backer board underneath the deck to prevent tearout. A carpenter's square helps keep your drill bit straight.

MAKE ROOM FOR SCREWHEADS
Use a countersink bit to trim the truck holes so that the bolts sit flush in the deck when the trucks are installed.

pro·file ROAROCKIT SKATEBOARD CO.

SK8MAKERS:
Ted Hunter and Norah Jackson

WHAT:
Roarockit Skateboard Co.

WHERE:
Toronto, Canada

WEBSITE:
www.roarockit.com

Ted Hunter and Norah Jackson might seem like unlikely champions of the DIY skateboard movement, but the two have single handedly democratized the business of skateboard making and sparked a tiny revolution in garage shops and skateparks around the globe.

The husband-and-wife duo are founders of Roarockit Skateboard Co., a Toronto-based startup that pioneered a process and the tools to build a high-quality skateboard deck from scratch. The mail-order kit they developed is safe and easy enough for kids to complete on a kitchen table in a long weekend.

It doesn't matter that Ted and Norah don't actually skate. Their business was founded on a philosophy that kids should learn to use their hands to make things from scratch—to give them confidence, keep them out of trouble, and instill in them an appreciation for the handmade. It's just a coincidence that a DIY skateboard deck is one of the best projects you could possibly conceive to achieve all of those ends.

FROM WOODSHOP TO SKATESHOP

Before the skateboard, Ted was a professor at Ontario College of Art and Design University. In addition to teaching, he created freestanding sculptures and curvy, complex wall art made from metal and wood. Through all his work, he was constantly inventing and improving on the technique and theories he was practicing.

In 2001 when a bout with bad health led Ted and Norah to the Hawaiian island of Maui for an extended stay. Ted made time to volunteer at the Hui No'eau Visual Arts Center, a local non-profit community center for artists, teaching a woodworking class for local teenagers. At Norah's suggestion, he settled on a project that combined his experience bending wood with a project the students could surely appreciate: skateboards.

ALL IN THE FAMILY
Husband and wife team Ted Hunter and Norah Jackson stand outside the Roarockit Skateboard Co. headquarters in Toronto, Canada.

SPREADING THE WORD
Ted Hunter got the idea for his Roarockit skateboard kit after teaching a woodworking class to students in Hawaii.

Ted didn't know anything about skateboards, so he headed to a local skate shop to do some research. He discovered a surprising fact: Some of the best skate decks on the market were constructed from Canadian maple sourced near his hometown and available at the lumber yard where he'd been buying wood for years.

He took home a skateboard deck and used it to reverse-engineer a one-sided mold. He placed an order from his hometown lumber yard for enough maple veneer for a shopful of kids and had it shipped to the small Hawaiian island thousands of miles away. He rigged up a vacuum press system just like the ones he used back home in his sculpture work. In front of a shop full of wide-eyed Hawaiian teenagers, lo and behold, it worked; The first Roarockit skateboard was created.

Over the next year, Ted got to work downsizing the project into an affordable, simple kit that could be packaged, shipped, unpacked, and completed pretty much anywhere by anyone, no matter their woodworking experience. But there was one bug he couldn't resolve: the pricey vacuum press pump that powered the system didn't fit in a box.

ALL PHOTOS COURTESY OF ROAROCKIT SKATEBOARD CO.

continued...

pro•file ROAROCKIT SKATEBOARD CO. continued

A FLEXIBLE TOOL
The vacuum bag that comes with the Roarockit kit can do more than just glue up skate decks. Its size and ease of use make it a great tool for freeform bending. No mold required, just extract the air and use your hands to bend the material into shape.

IN A PREVIOUS LIFE
Before the skateboard, Ted Hunter used vacuum veneering techniques to produce curvy and complex wood sculptures, like the one pictured above combining wood and mixed materials.

The ah-ha moment came over a glass of wine in his living room. Ted saw his wife using a hand-powered vacuum pump to pull air from a half-empty wine bottle to keep it fresh. It could pump the air from a vacuum bag, too. He rigged up a vacuum bag to test out the theory and it worked. Paired up with some maple veneer, a foam mold, and a few extra supplies, the kit now contained everything needed to make a skateboard, and it fit in a tidy box.

They quickly took the kit to market, winning a method patent from the U.S. and Canadian patent and trademark offices, and winning customers and fans around the globe.

Ted had solved a major dilemma that had held back garage-shop skatemaking from really taking off. He figured out a super-simple way to produce a pro-quality deck that didn't involve expensive, heavy equipment.

The second nut he cracked was opening up access to the high-quality maple veneers used to produce a skateboard deck. Until Ted and Norah put the material up for sale on their website, skateboard veneer was not easy to find or buy in small quantities. The big deck makers were producing the veneers themselves, or buying it from suppliers in huge quantities.

With his lumber yard connections and proximity to the source, Ted didn't have to look hard or far to find a supplier of maple veneers that he

CUSTOM IS KING
A row of custom skate decks adorns the walls at Roarockit Skateboard Co. headquarters in Toronto, Canada.

could resell at a reasonable price. His hope was to get as many people as he could building skateboard decks and practicing his method with his kit. If he was successful, he would need a lot of wood.

GOING UP?
A flight of stairs at Roarockit Skateboard Co. headquarters in Toronto, Canada, constructed from a series of custom skate decks.

BUILDING A DIY-SKATEBOARD COMMUNITY

The Roarockit kit has given root to a diverse, global community of garage-shop skateboard builders—creative and ambitous skaters who are crafty with power tools; handy dads who want to spend time with their kids in their shop and build something other than a birdhouse; teachers and educators looking to ignite a creative spark in their students with a project they can relate to.

Supporting a global community of makers with tools, materials, and inspiration has helped Ted and Norah build a thriving business with a purpose, and they're leaving a legacy of handmade skateboards in their wake.

ALL PHOTOS COURTESY OF ROAROCKIT SKATEBOARD CO.

CHAPTER 7

HOW TO BUILD A CUSTOM SKATEBOARD TO YOUR OWN SPECS

Chances are, building your first Roarockit skateboard will only fire you up to make more. It's a slippery slope, and soon enough you'll feel the urge to expand your designs beyond the three pre-cut kits you can buy online. In this chapter, I'll show you how to up your game by using the Roarockit method to produce a custom deck of your own shape, size, and contour.

To demonstrate the process start to finish, I packed up a box of vacuum bags, molds, and maple veneer and headed to Community Woodshop, an awesome open studio for woodworking in Los Angeles, where five newbies joined in on a group build over the course of three days.

Four students built Roarockit kits, and a fifth chose a more ambitious route—to design and build a custom deck of his own size, shape, and contour. The design was inspired by 1980s skateboard decks from brands like Powell-Peralta and Santa Cruz Skateboards. They were some of the earliest boards built to go vertical. The deck in this chapter features a kick on the tail and the nose, with some concave on the rails. It's longer than the standard modern skateboard deck. It's also wider—up to 9-¼ in. at its widest—leaving plenty of room to plant your feet when battling gravity.

the goods

TOOLS
Bandsaw or jigsaw, stationary belt sander, backsaw, 4-in-1 combination rasp/file, Stanley Surform, block plane, drill-driver, ¼-in. drill bit, countersink bit, hand sanding block.

MATERIALS
Seven sheets of 1⁄16-in. maple veneer (five long-grain, two cross grain), PVA wood glue, polyurethane wood finish.

EQUIPMENT
Thin Air Press vacuum bag, hand pump, foam block, paint roller, dust mask, safety glasses.

ACCESSORIES
Trucks and wheels (size may vary depending on the shape and size of your finished deck), bearings, risers, grip tape.

A CUSTOM DESIGN
Create a one-of-a-kind skateboard deck using the Roarockit method by shaping your own foam mold and cutting out the deck with a shape of your own design.

custom skate deck

Create a custom skateboard tailored to fit your specific dimensions using the same hand-pump-powered vacuum bag kit demonstrated in Chapter 6; only this time ditch the pre-cut veneers and pre-shaped foam mold and start from scratch.

LENGTH:
33 ½ in.

WIDTH:
9 ½ in.

WHEEL SPAN:
15 ½ in.

MATERIALS:
Seven layers 1⁄16 in. maple veneer

TRUCKS:
Independent 159

BEARINGS:
Bones Super REDS

WHEELS:
Sector 9 59 mm

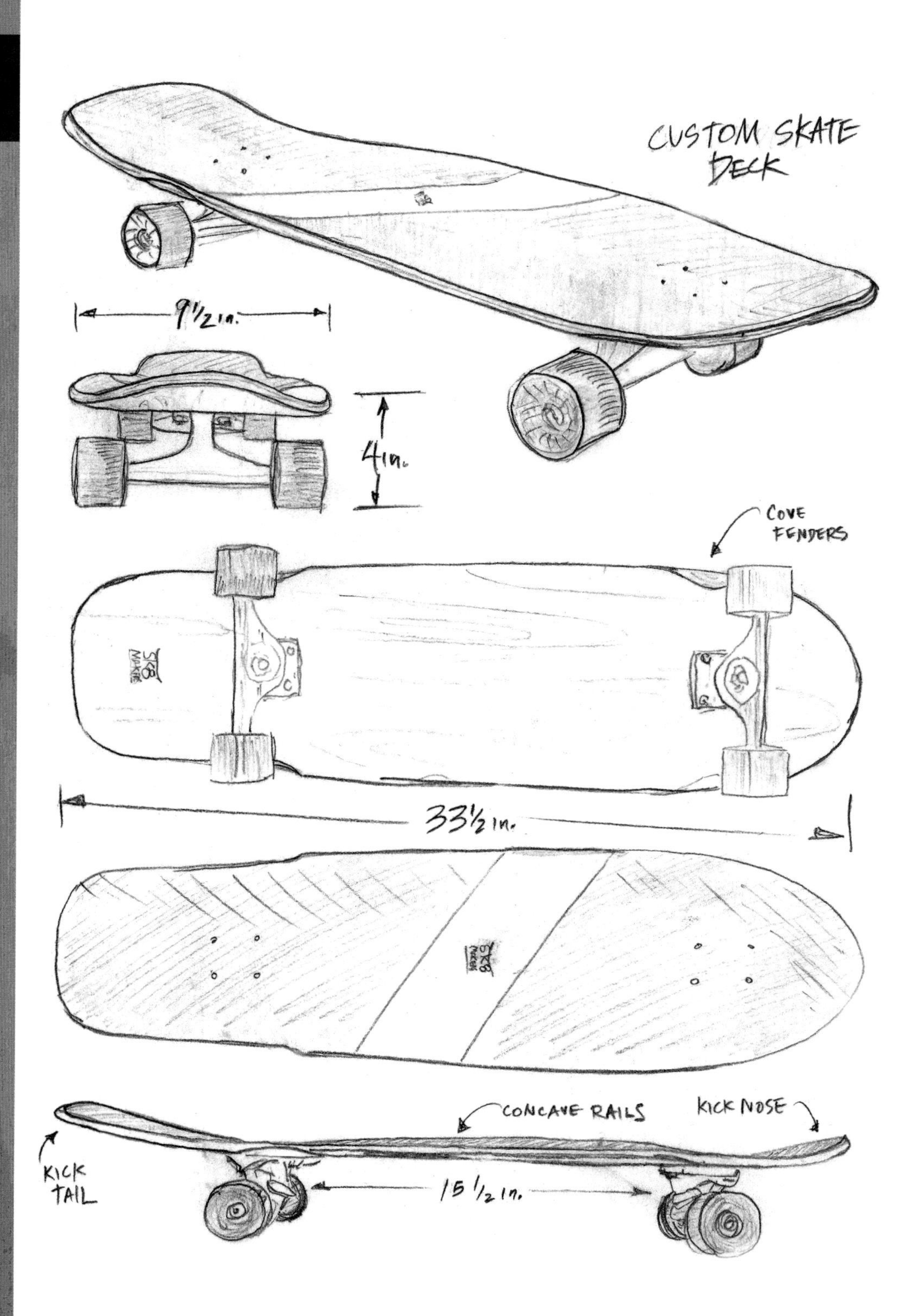

CUT THE FOAM TO SIZE
A sharp backsaw is a great tool for cutting the foam block to width, length, and contour. Before cutting into the foam block, mark it with a centerline and use a paper template to trace the deck shape onto one side. Mark perpendicular lines to indicate the start of the bend at each end of the board.

A PERFECT INVERSE
With all of your lines marked on the foam mold, the next step is to shape it to the inverse contour of the finished skate deck.

CREATE A TEMPLATE FOR THE THIRD DIMENSION

Same as always: The first step in designing your custom deck is to draw out the deck shape and create a full-size template. Only this time, unlike the flat hackboard deck, you also need to design for the third dimension to define the bend for the kick tail, kick nose, and concave along each side.

Start by drawing the birds-eye view outline of the deck with a centerline. Then mark perpendicular lines across the width of the deck where you want the kick to begin at the nose and the tail. For this particular deck design, I measured about 3 in. back from the nose and about 6 in. back from the tail. Then use those same measurements to create a side view template. This

GIVE IT A SHAVE

Carve away at the tapered curve with a utility knife. Even better, use a Stanley Surform cutting tool from a Roarockit Kit to shave away the foam like a cheese grater.

profile template allows you to define the angle of the kick in the tail and nose, and to mark out the beginning and end points of the concave along each side.

When you're happy with your deck templates, it's time to transfer all of these lines to a 2-in.-thick foam block so you can shape it to the final mold. It's important to start with a foam block that measures the same width and length as the sheets of maple veneer. When you're laminating a stack of uncut veneers to a foam mold, it's important to not let the veneers overhang the foam blank during glue-up. Overhang can prevent the wood from forming perfectly to the mold and could leave you with unintended bumps and dips. Conversely, starting with veneers that are shorter and narrower than the foam mold makes it hard to align the pieces once the glue is applied and the stack is in the vacuum bag.

Draw all of the top-view dimensions on the top surface of the foam mold. Then mark the side view on each side. Finally, mark for the concave. This line runs parallel to the edge of the mold and begins and ends with an arc at the front and back wheels. At its widest in the center, the line measures about 2½ in. from the edge.

WORK OUT THE CURVES

Start by defining the kicktail and kick nose. Use the lines drawn on the top and sides of the mold to guide your cut. Next, shape the mold for the concave on the side rails. This requires more sculpting since there is a taper at each end. Use the saw to remove the bulk of the material.

SMOOTH IT OUT

When the foam mold is rough-cut to shape, sand the mold smooth with 150-grit sandpaper. A chunk of foam cutoff serves as a great sanding block. Make sure that you shape the mold evenly on the left and right sides, otherwise your deck will end up lopsided.

ASSEMBLE THE DECK

If you've assembled a Roarockit kit before, you now the rules: apply an even coat of glue on both surfaces of the joining veneer and get the stack into the bag and sealed in seven minutes or less. Then pump out the air and let the glue dry for at least eight hours. If you're jumping into this project as your first build, read through the vacuum veneering sections on pages 96-101 of the Chapter 6, "How to build a Skate Deck from a Kit."

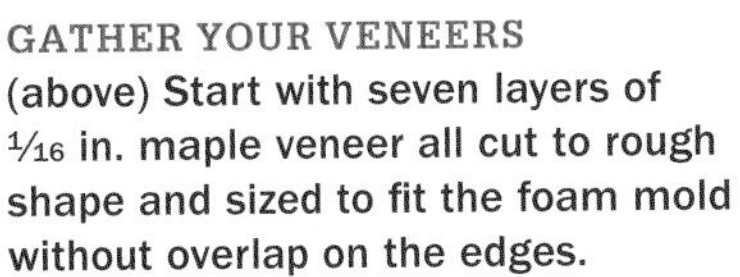

GATHER YOUR VENEERS
(above) Start with seven layers of $\frac{1}{16}$ in. maple veneer all cut to rough shape and sized to fit the foam mold without overlap on the edges.

ROLL IT ON
(left) The key to a good lamination is applying just the right amount of glue to the veneer layers. Using a paint roller helps achieve consistent coverage.

ALL PITCH IN
Students at Community Woodshop team up to glue the maple veneers before laminating a skateboard deck using the Roarockit method.

PUMP IT OUT
The standard Roarockit bag and pump works even on custom designs of this size. With more hands at work you can glue up all of the layers at once. A few extra hands never hurts—although, admittedly, this is comical overkill.

SHAPE THE DECK

Once the glue has dried, un-bag your blank and you're ready to cut it to shape. Start with the same paper template you created earlier. Simply draw out the design and cut it to shape. Similar to the hackboard project, you could cut out the shape using a handheld jigsaw. But since we had access to a full woodshop for this build, I chose a much faster and more accurate route: to cut it out using a bandsaw and shape it on a stationary belt and disc sander.

A bandsaw is one of the most versatile stationary power tools in the workshop. It can cut straight lines or curvy ones, and it has an adjustable table and fence to accommodate a wide variety of dimensioned lumber. Using a bandsaw is also the easiest way to cut out the deck shape on your glued-up blank.

Just like when you're using a jigsaw, when cutting to a line on the bandsaw stay about 1⁄16-in. outside of the line—and whatever you do, don't let the blade cross it. You can always remove waste later with sanders, but once you cut past the line, you can't add material.

MARK OUT THE SHAPE
After removing the blank deck from the vacuum bag, mark out the shape of the deck with the template.

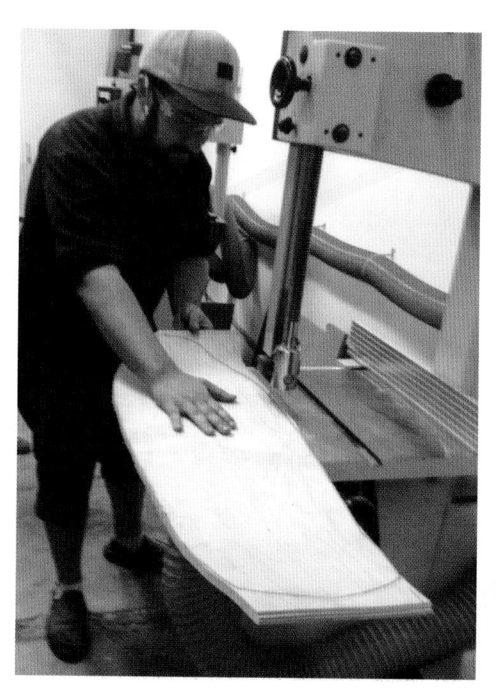

CUT IT TO SHAPE
Cut out the deck shape on the bandsaw, making sure to stay about 1⁄16-in. outside the line. Hold the deck securely to the bandsaw table to prevent rocking as you cut the curves.

As you cut you'll notice that the curves of the deck offer a bit of a challenge. To handle sharp curves, make relief cuts anywhere along the shape where the blade will have trouble making the turn. Also, make sure to hold the deck securely as you cut. This will enable you to keep the deck stable on the bandsaw table and prevent the deck from rocking back and forth as you cut.

Once the deck is cut to rough size, use a combination of power sanders and hand tools to get it to its final shape. As always when shaping a deck, first define the perimeter of the deck by creating a perfectly square edge all the way around. Once you've worked out all the bumps and dips and faired all of the curves, round-over the top and bottom edges to create the bullnose edge.

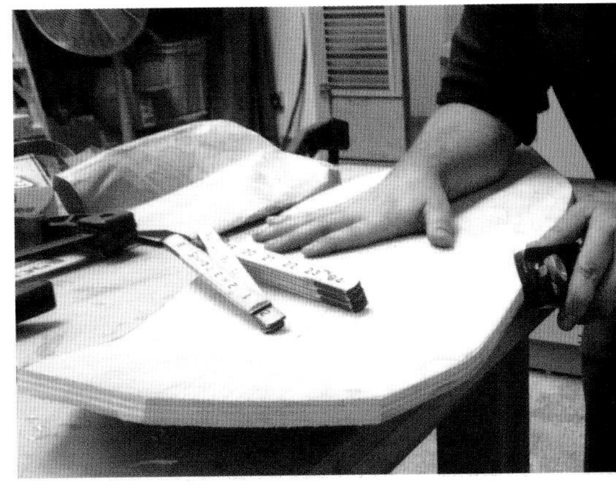

CLEAN UP THE EDGES
When it comes to final finishing on the edge, nothing beats an old fashioned block plane for creating straight lines and fair curves.

POWER SAND FAIR CURVES
If you have access to a stationary belt and disc sander, use them. These machines work quickly to remove the excess waste and refine your deck shape.

MAKE A FOOLPROOF TEMPLATE FOR DRILLING TRUCK HOLES

Rather than marking out the holes on the deck one at a time with each new skateboard you make, you can speed up the process by creating a reusable template that positions the holes right where you want them. I made mine with scraps of clear acrylic, but you can use whatever found materials you have laying around. The idea is to spend all your effort marking and drilling holes in the correct spot once so that you can quickly cut holes in every board thereafter.

Here's a simple method to make a template that doesn't require complicated layout. You'll need a sheet of acrylic available at any hardware store or home center, a 3/8-in. drill bit intended for cutting plastic, a straight edge ruler, and any pair of skate trucks.

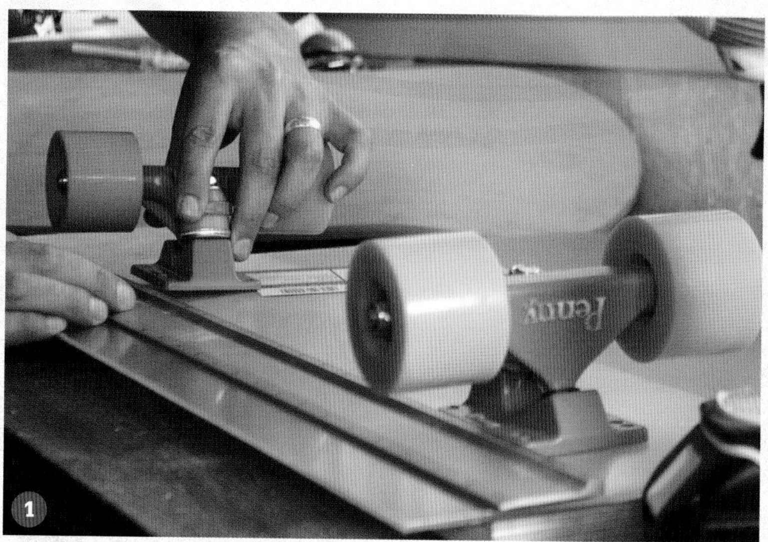

1 LINE UP THE TRUCKS
Place a matching set of trucks on top of a sheet of acrylic at least as long as the span of your skateboard deck. Push the trucks against a straight edge for perfect alignment.

2 SET YOUR SPAN
Measure the span from the front truck hole on each deck by lining up the center of each hole with a mark on your ruler.

3 START DRILLING
Place a piece of scrap wood under the deck where the drill bit will exit, then drill through your skateboard truck hole into the acrylic. Hold the truck steady as you go until the bit hits the scrap wood.

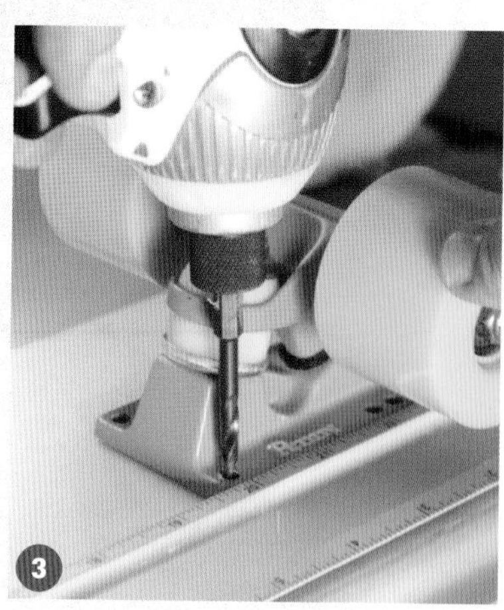

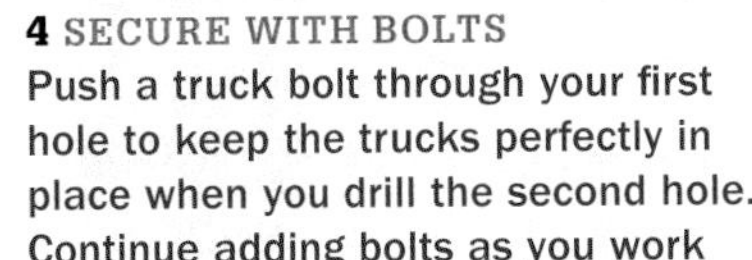

4 SECURE WITH BOLTS
Push a truck bolt through your first hole to keep the trucks perfectly in place when you drill the second hole. Continue adding bolts as you work your way through all four holes.

5 SECOND TRUCK, SAME AS THE FIRST
Same process on the other end. Align the truck against the straight edge and drill each hole, pinning them with bolts as you go.

6 FIND YOUR CENTER
Mark a centerline down the length of the template to help you align the template on a skate deck later on.

7 MARK A CENTERLINE
Line up a straight edge on your marked center points and scribe a line down the center of your template with a razor.

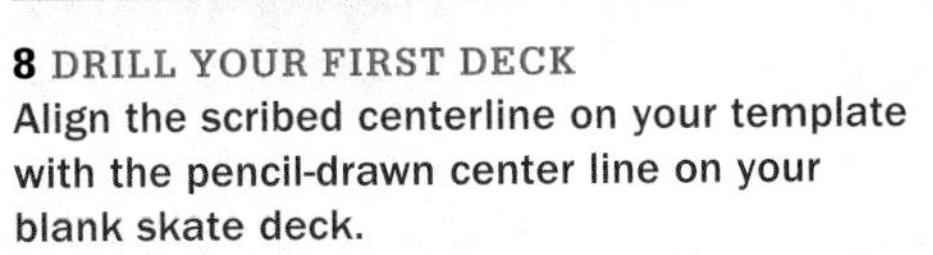

8 DRILL YOUR FIRST DECK
Align the scribed centerline on your template with the pencil-drawn center line on your blank skate deck.

9 CLAMP WHILE YOU CUT
Clamp the template in place and drill all eight holes. Remember to place a piece of scrap wood beneath the deck to prevent tear-out where the drill bit exits the cut.

MARK OUT THE HOLES
(right) Determine the distance between truck holes by comparing holes on the RockitRuler to those on your actual trucks. Then center the RockitRuler on your deck using the diamond cutout and then mark out the four corresponding holes.

DRILL THEM OUT
Choose a drill bit that allows your truck bolt to slide though but doesn't allow any wobble. Use a scrap of wood as a backer board to prevent the bit from tearing out wood fibers as it exits the board.

A REUSABLE TEMPLATE FOR LOCATING TRUCK HOLES

The last step is to locate the truck holes and drill and countersink. If you've been bitten by the DIY skateboard bug and have the urge to make multiple decks, you'll quickly discover that it helps to make templates to speed up repetitive tasks like this. To learn how to make a simple template that will allow you to layout truck holes quickly and accurately on any deck, see "Make a Foolproof Template for Drilling Truck Holes" on pages 118-119.

The concept works so well the folks at Roarockit Skateboard Co. teamed up with a local skateboard builder named Shaun Bunder to make a commercial tool just like it called the "RockitRuler." It's a specialized ruler with a few different elements that makes it extremely useful for custom skateboard makers. Equally spaced holes spanning the ruler allow you to easily locate and mark the location of the truck holes at any distance. Diamond-shaped cutouts running along the center of the ruler help you center the holes on the board.

After you've marked the location of the holes and before you drill them, use a center punch to mark a dimple in the wood. This will help guide the drill bit to ensure that you cut your holes exactly where you want them. Be sure to use a backer board when drilling through the deck to prevent tear-out where the bit exits the back of the cut.

Finally, give the deck a final sanding, apply finish, and set up your deck with grip tape and trucks.

MAKE ROOM FOR BOLT HEADS
Once the holes are drilled, use a simple countersink bit to hog out a recess that will allow the bolt heads to sit flush or slightly recessed above the top of the deck.

ADD AN AGGRESSIVE BEND
To make the radical bends required on a drop-through deck, it takes a little more coaxing than a vacuum veneer bag. Once the bag is pumped dry, wood cauls and clamps are applied to help complete the sharpest bends.

USE WHATEVER IT TAKES.
(below) When one set of cauls isn't enough, simply add more. Notice that the form in this case is simply a rounded length of wood over which the wood is bent.

EXPERIMENT WITH YOUR OWN EXTREME BUILDS

Some custom skateboard builds can incorporate extreme bends. While the bends may seem impossible at a glance, they're actually pretty easy to achieve. In most cases all you need—beyond the Roarockit vacuum bag system—is a little extra muscle to coax the stack of veneers to the shape of the form. One approach is to reinforce the assembly with clamps on the outside of the vacuum bag and distribute the pressure with wood cauls.

Once all of the air has been extracted from the bag, place cauls on both sides of the bend. Be sure to sand down the corners on the cauls so they don't tear into the vacuum bag when tightening the clamps.

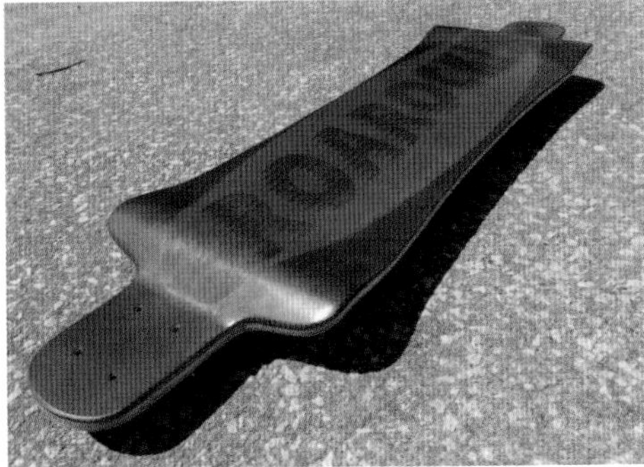

DOWNHILL READY
(left) A batch of custom drop-through decks featuring unconventional bends and trucks designed for downhill bombing awaits final shaping and finishing at the Roarockit Skateboard Co. in Toronto, Canada. (above) The same design has received a painted finish.

pro·file CHILLER DECKS

WEBSITE:
efinewoodworking.com

SK8MAKER:
Mark Edmundson

WHERE:
Sandpoint, Idaho

FEATURED DECK:
Mountain Snow Skates

Fine furniture maker Mark Edmundson is an unsuspecting innovator in the world of custom skateboard making. From his rural workshop in Sandpoint, Idaho, Edmundson has built hundreds of custom decks designed for a very unique purpose—shredding snowy hillsides.

An accomplished furniture maker, woodworking teacher, author, and hardcore back-country snow sports enthusiast, Edmundson has taken the custom deck-building process to a new level with his "snowskates," a combination skateboard and snowboard with a touch of surfboard thrown in to provide a free-footed ride over snowy terrain.

As an early innovator in the action snow sport of "mountain skating," Edmundson experimented with a variety of concepts and eventually launched Chiller Decks, a part-time business and full-time obsession.

Here's how it works: A rider stands free-footed on a large custom skateboard deck designed by Edmundson in his shop. That deck is then

"SNOW" BOARDS
Designed for shredding your way across the snowscape, the design for these unique "snowskates" is inspired by skateboards and snowboards, with even a little surfboard thrown into the mix.

attached to a lower snow skate that operates more like a wide ski or snowboard. The two parts are connected with a custom metal binding that allows the rider to steer the board like a skateboard on snow. A leash ties the rider to the deck to keep them connected during spills and wipeouts.

Edmundson does his prototyping and design work using a vacuum press and one-part mold. It's the fastest and most efficient way to test out new shapes and designs, he says. But once he settles on a final design, he turns his prototype into a two-sided concrete mold for his shop-made hydraulic press, affectionately dubbed the "Hillbilly Press."

It works just like the hydraulic presses at large skateboard manufacturing facilities, except it's cobbled together from scrap steel, plywood, and concrete.

FREESTYLE SNOW SKATING
Mark Edmundson catches air in the back country near his snowy Idaho home and workshop.

ALL PHOTOS COURTESY OF MARK EDMUNDSON

continued...

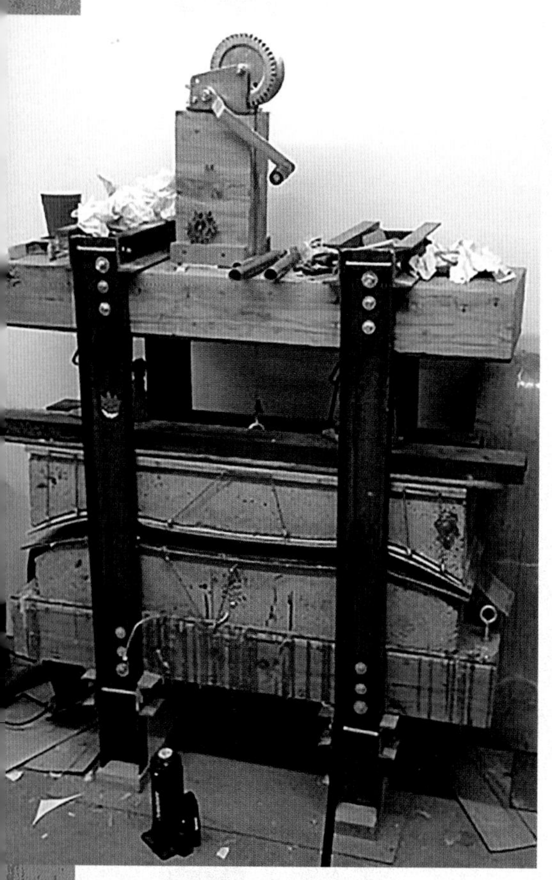

THE HILLBILLY PRESS
(above and right) Modeled after a two-part industrial press, Edmundson's "Hillbilly Press" is made of scrap materials and a heavy two-part concrete mold that Edmundson created himself.

MAKE YOUR OWN HILLBILLY PRESS

The first step to making your own Hillbilly Press is pouring the two-part concrete molds. Start with a rectangular skateboard blank created using a one-sided mold and vacuum press. Lay it on edge and build a box around it that's as long and as tall as it, and about 18 in. wide.

Attach a piece of plywood on one side of the box to contain the wet concrete. Then install two heavy-duty bolts on both sides of the mold, so when the concrete sets the bolts will be buried inside it. Lay a few pieces of rebar inside the concrete to strengthen the mold for long-term use. After the concrete has set, disassemble the box to reveal your top and bottom concrete forms.

Finally, build an H-frame structure to support the concrete forms that includes a pulley system to raise and lower the top of the mold during the lamination process. This task isn't complicated, but requires a mechanical brain and some basic metalworking skills.

HOT OFF THE PRESS
(above) A stack of Chiller Deck parts awaits the next step in the woodworking process.

THE MOLD FITS THE BOARD
An assortment of Chiller Decks in various sizes rest next to the shop-made molds that are used to shape them during the lamination process.

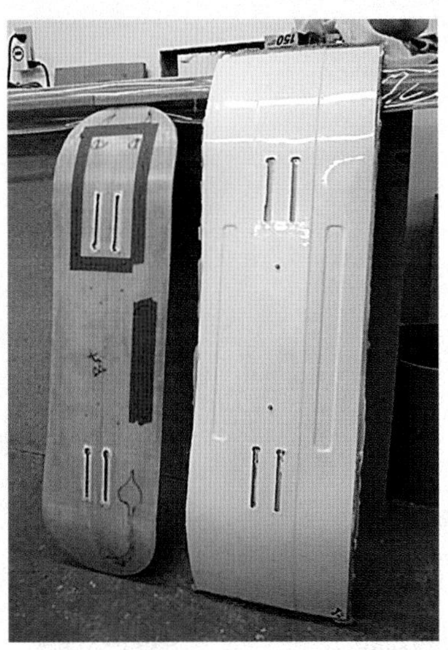

ONE-OF-A-KIND DESIGN
(above) A set of templates is used to cut out the housing for the bindings on the ski.

THE TWO-PART DESIGN IS THE KEY
A Chiller Deck is composed of two parts: the freestanding skate deck on top and the ski on the bottom that makes contact with the snowy terrain.

A MARRIAGE OF SKATE AND SKI
A special binding system that attaches the deck to the ski makes for a smooth and fluid ride.

ALL PHOTOS COURTESY OF MARK EDMUNDSON

CHAPTER 8

PRO TIPS

ADD SPEED, SCALE, & ACCURACY

When DIY skateboard makers moved out of their garages and into the factory, they introduced a whole new level of consistency and exactness to the deck-building process thanks to precision tooling and factory automation. This has helped push the sport of skateboarding to new heights, literally. Pro riders rely on the extreme exactness in the weight, shape, and ergonomics of a deck to pull off their death-defying tricks on a half pipe or in a skate park. Change one element of the deck—a steeper tail kick, a wider wheel base—and you can easily throw a skater off his game.

If your goal as a skatemaker is to produce skateboard decks in quantity and achieve consistent results each time—whether as a hobby or a business—you'll need to employ some of the same concepts in your garage shop that professionals employ in the factory. In this chapter we'll look at a few techniques used by professional furniture makers and skateboard makers that you can adopt for your own skatemaking workshop.

SCALING THE OPERATION
You don't have to run a factory to produce quality skateboard decks in quantity. A stack of unfinished decks (left) sits in wait at District Skates in downtown Los Angeles. With a few pro tools and techniques you can create a mini production line your own garage or small shop.

the goods

TOOLS
Bandsaw, planer, jointer, table saw, drill press, veneer saw or utility knife.

MATERIALS
1⁄16-in. maple veneer, PVA wood glue, veneer tape, latex paint.

EQUIPMENT
Workbench, vacuum pump and table, laser cutter, wood burning tools, branding iron.

ACCESSORIES
Skateboard trucks for sizing and laying out truck holes.

A SMALL SHOP WILL DO
Here I'm hard at work in SK8Makers HQ, a small corner of my detached garage. All it takes are some basic tools and equipment and a sturdy workbench with a bench vice. A little natural light helps, too.

BUILD THE ULTIMATE SKATEMAKERS WORKSHOP

Most of us will only ever have the chance to build skateboard decks in our garage and basement workshops, jamming our tools and materials into tiny spaces shared with cars and bicycles and camping gear or washers and dryers. We all make do, but we dream of bigger spaces filled with power tools that can accomplish any operation against wood that we might wish upon it: chop, slice, shave, shape, sand, smooth.

A good shop starts with a good space—something that's roomy enough to fit all of our your tools and with adequate power and good light. Access is also something to consider: You may have a ton of space in your basement or garage loft, but can you easily transport a sheet of plywood to it? How about a new 1,000-lb. tablesaw?

If you're like me when I first started building, your budget probably doesn't have room for all the tools that could belong in the perfect woodshop. Most of those lucky enough to acquire the supreme collection do it over the long haul, investing in one tool at a time as new projects require it.

The most essential of these tools to buy and in which order is hotly debated, but in my book (and this literally is my book) here's how the dream shop of tools lines up from first buy to last.

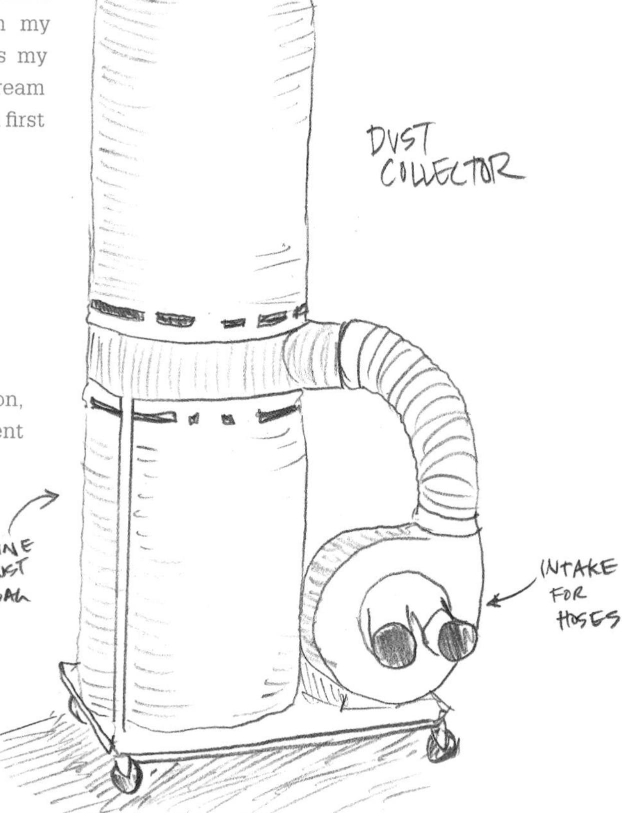

1. DON'T SKIMP ON DUST COLLECTION

A good shop is a safe shop, fully stocked with eye protection, hearing protection, first-aid kits, and, most importantly, a sufficient air filtration and dust-collection system. These days, too much is known about the harmful effects of fine wood dust on human lungs. The tiny particles released from power tools and sanders can cause microscopic and irreparable damage each time they're inhaled. Wood dust is also an irritant that can trigger an allergic reaction. Potentially, it's even a carcinogen. Small shops can get by using a portable shop vacuum to clean up the dust one tool at a time, but fully-equipped woodshops with multiple machines require a a powerful dust-collection system with 4-in. diameter hoses and fittings for maximum suck. Do your research to make sure your shop space stays dust-free.

2. THE TABLESAW

Perhaps the greatest workhorse of any woodworking shop is the tablesaw, a powerful, precision woodworking machine that can slice through almost any chunk of wood to cut it down to shape, size, and dimension. Tablesaws are designed to do a few cuts really well and some cuts not at all. An adjustable rip fence that moves along the tabletop is used to cut long boards or sheetgoods into narrower strips. A tablesaw's miter fence is used to cross-cut lengths of wood. The blade tilts and the miter fence adjusts, so you can cut at an angle or on a bevel.

Tablesaws come in three basic sizes: the smallest and least powerful are the portable tablesaws, designed to be transported to a carpenter's job site. At the high end are cabinet saws, heavy-duty stationary machines that can rip through the hardest of woods. Somewhere in between is the hybrid tablesaw, which offers the precision of a cabinet saw in a smaller package. Buy the best you can afford and you'll have it forever.

A tablesaw can be your best companion in the shop, but it can also be dangerous. Protect yourself from kickback by using a modern blade guard and riving knife, a safety accessory that prevents the wood from catching on the blade and flying through the air like a bullet. Keep your hands and arms clear of the blade's path at all times. Finally, don't wear jewelry or loose clothing when operating a tablesaw.

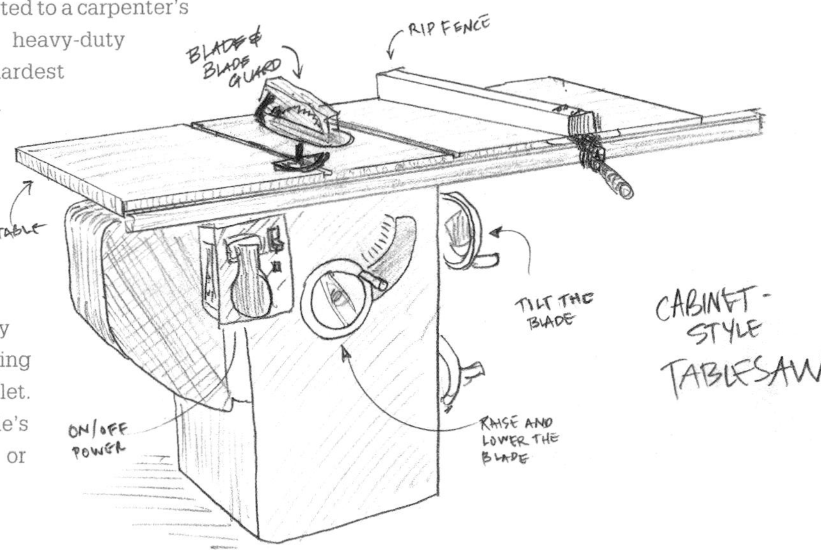

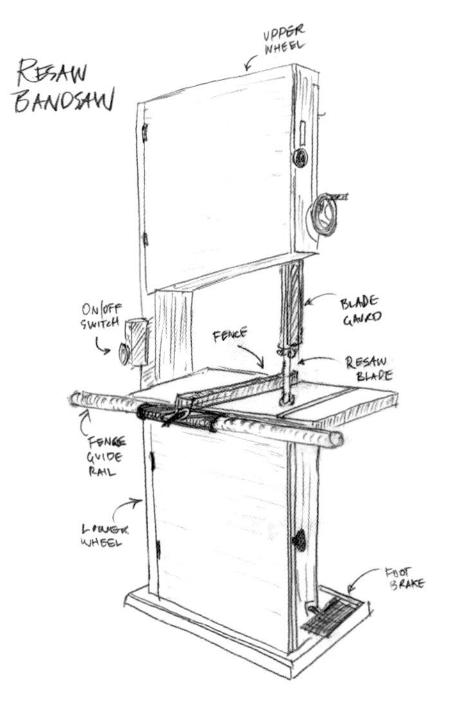

3. THE BANDSAW COMES IN TWO SIZES

Right up there with the tablesaw in usefulness is the trusty bandsaw, one of the most versatile cutting tools in the shop. You can choose from a variety of blades designed for different materials and operations. Bandsaws can cut straight lines, curves, sharp corners, and stopped cuts. An adustable table and fence allow you perform any of those operations at an angle. Paired with shopmade jigs and fixtures, it can do a lot more. Most shops can get by with a standard 14-in. bandsaw. But if you want to equip your shop with a tool that can resaw wide boards into paper-thin sheets of veneer, you'll need at least an 18-in. bandsaw with a wide, sharp blade designed for resawing wood.

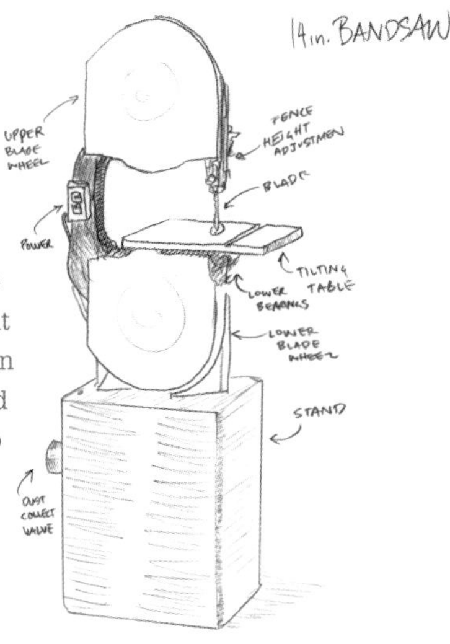

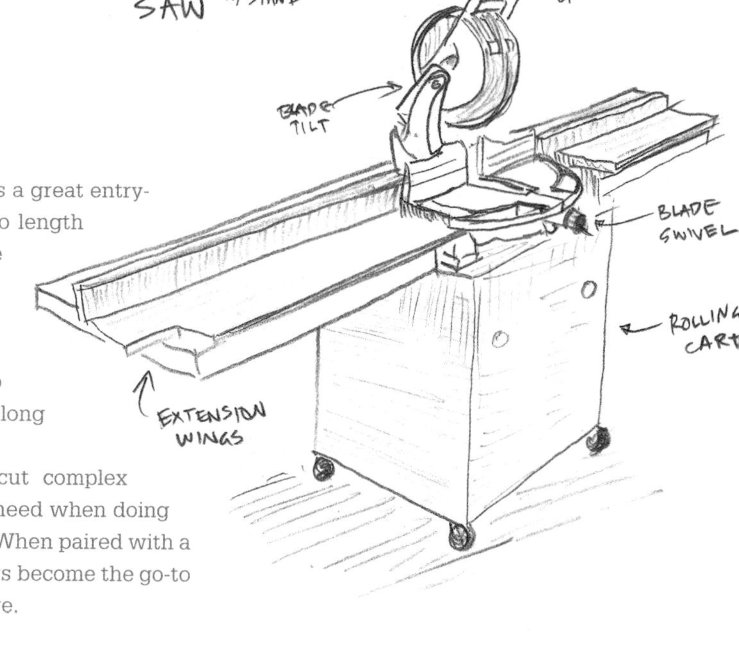

4. SLIDING COMPOUND MITER SAW

Sometimes called a chop saw, this portable power tool is a great entry-level power tool designed to cut long pieces of wood to length or at a combination of angles. They comes in three varieties—at the low end is the standard miter with a pivoting blade. Next up is the compound miter saw that has a blade that both pivots and tilts. At the high end is the sliding compound miter saw, which has the two other adjustments as well as a sliding blade that slides along a track to cross-cut wide boards.

This trifecta of settings allows the operator to cut complex compound angles at precise measurements, a common need when doing projects like installing trim or crown molding in a home. When paired with a commercial stand or a shopmade workstation, these saws become the go-to tool for any quick cutting operations your projects require.

5. JOINTER AND PLANER ARE A TEAM

Constructing things from wood is almost impossible if you don't start with boards that are flat and square. Rarely is lumberyard stock as straight and square as you need. If possible, buy lumber that is rough-sawn, meaning that it comes in thicker pieces with extra material which the jointer and planer remove during the squaring process. Rough-sawn stock is also less expensive.

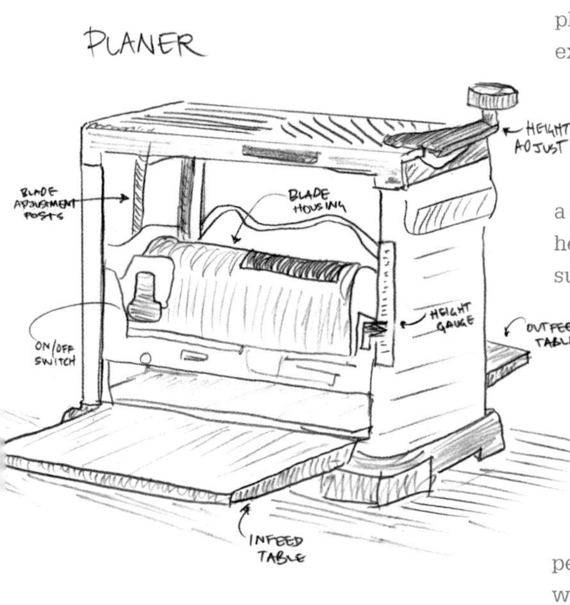

The jointer and planer work hand-in-hand to dimension, flatten, and square lumber. A jointer is designed to flatten the the face and edges of a board. Jointers come in a range of sizes with cutting capacities from 6-in. wide to more than 13-in. wide. A jointer has four main components: a spinning blade (or cutterhead); an in-feed table set slightly lower than the height of the cutterhead; an out-feed table set equal to the cutter height to support the wood as it exits the cut; and a fence to help guide the board (usually at a perfect 90°). To flatten a face or edge, simply run it across the cutterhead from infeed to outfeed table using the fence as your guide.

A thickness planer cuts the top and bottom faces of a board, either to flatten it and remove bumps and dips, or to make the piece of wood thinner. A planer that can accommodate lumber up to 13 in. wide and 2 in. thick is perfectly adequate for most woodshops. These entry-level models are often referred to as "lunchbox planers" because of their size and shape. The wider and thicker you yout lumber you intend to use, the larger and more expensive your planer will be.

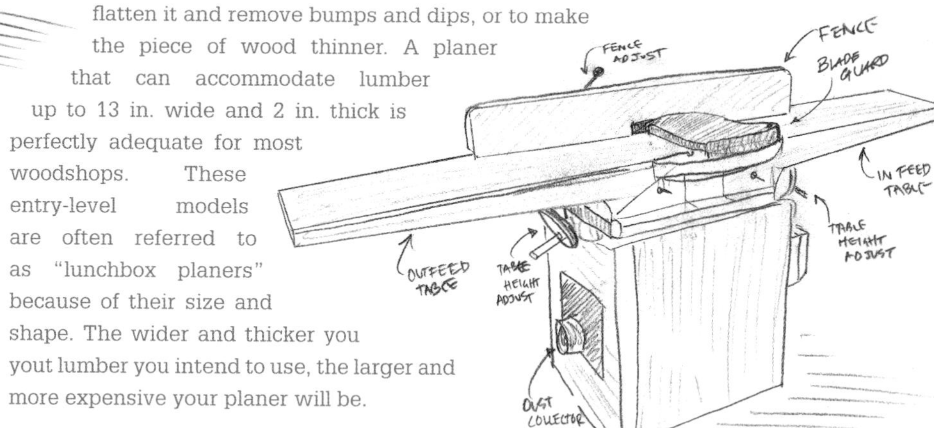

6. VARIABLE-SPEED ROUTER AND ROUTER TABLE

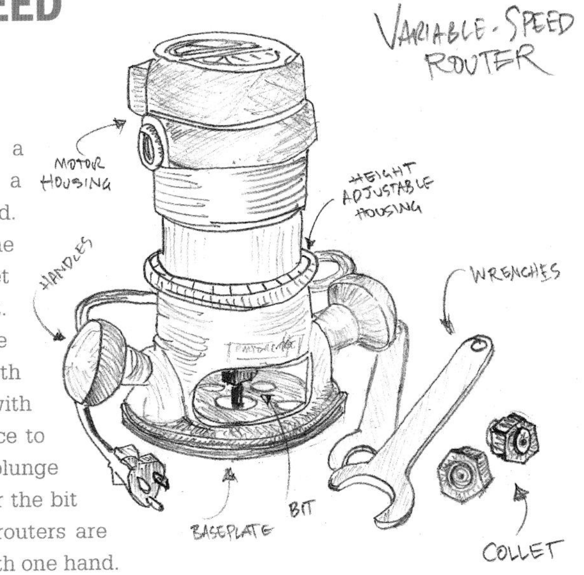

Put simply, a router is a handheld motor that spins a cutting bit that shapes wood. The bit attaches to the motor's shaft using a collet to secure the shank of the bit. The most common routers are large enough to require both hands to operate. They come with a fixed base that locks in place to cut edges or a spring-loaded plunge base that allows you to lower the bit into the wood. Smaller trim routers are light enough to maneuver with one hand.

Most router bits are used to trim the edge of a piece of wood into a specific shape, like the round-over on a skateboard deck. Other bits cut grooves or trim edges flush. Large-diameter bits usually have a ½-in. dia. shank but smaller bits can get by with a ¼-in. dia. shank. Raise or lower the bit to set the depth of your cut and set the speed of the router to between 10,000 RPM and 30,000 RPM—heavier cuts require slower speeds.

When paired with a router table, the router can serve as one of the best tools in your shop for shaping decks quickly and accurately. A router table can be bought or easily made out of plywood. Remove the base plate on your router and use the screws to mount it underneath the router table so that the bit extends above the table's surface. Introduce a bearing-guided, flush-trim bit into the picture and you're ready to start mass producing skate decks. A bearing on the bit rides the edge of a template to guide the bit. Attach a template to your workpiece and the bit will cut it to the exact shape of the template.

7. THE DRILL PRESS

Want to drill a straight, round hole in your skate deck? Buy a drill press. A big upgrade from a handheld power drill-driver, these tools are common in classic industrial woodshops and metal shops because they can be used to drill holes of any size and depth in both materials. A drill press is powered by a slow-speed motor that connects to a drill shaft with belts and pulleys. At the other end of the shaft is a chuck that can be tightened and loosened to hold a variety of drill bits. An adjustable table lets you easily raise and lower the depth of the drilled hole.

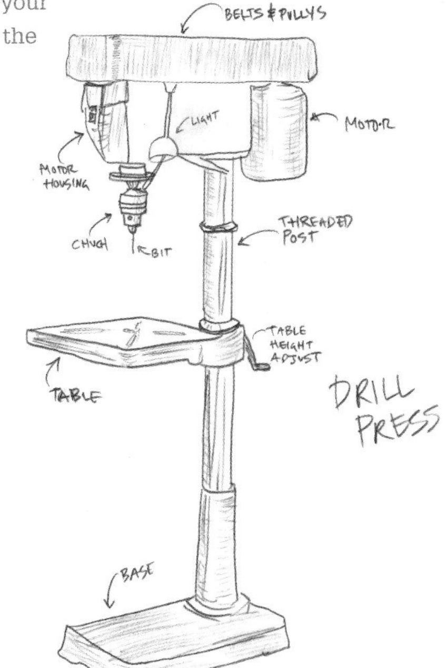

SPECIALIZED TOOL DRILLS EIGHT HOLES IN ONE!

Drilling consistent truck holes that are perfectly located is key to producing a quality board. Even when you make or buy templates it becomes a chore to drill all eight holes on a large number of decks. Tackling this process with a handheld drill, or even a drill press, the maker has eight opportunities to fail.

Somewhere along the way, some smart dude at a skateboard factory engineered a way to ensure perfect accuracy by cutting eight truck holes in a single pull. The result is a specialized drill press that operates two drill heads, each outfitted with four drill bits. Each drill head can be adjusted to handle different wheel spans. A series of clamps holds a stack of decks perfectly centered and aligned while the operator lowers the drill heads, cutting all eight holes at once.

Unfortunately, you won't find a multi-bit drill press at your local home center. Troll classifieds and machinery auctions to find one, or special order one at a hefty price.

TAKE OUT THE GUESSWORK
Want to know how to drill eight perfect truck holes in a custom skate deck? Find yourself one of these industrial drill presses that can drill eight holes in one pull.

DRILL ALL YOUR TRUCK HOLES AT ONCE
The eight-bit drill press is actually made up of two units that bore four clean, perfectly placed holes simultaneously.

8. STATIONARY POWER SANDERS

Not every woodshop bothers to stock a stationary disc and belt sander, and especially few will have the more specialized spindle sander on hand—even fewer of them not gathering dust. That's because power sanders like these have specialized uses for fairing curves in wood, rounding edges, and sculpting three-dimensional forms into a cloud of saw dust. But as you've seen in a few of the skateboard projects covered in this book, these high-speed, tough-grit sanders can take care of an otherwise tedious and time-consuming job in a flash. If you plan to run a small business shaping skate decks and coved fenders, investing in a stationary disc and belt sander and a spindle sander will pay off in the long run.

Handheld belt sanders are another skateshop staple thanks to their ability to sand away large amounts of material fast. A front and back handle also make it useful for shaping and sculpting wood. Belt sanders come in a few sizes, measured by the width of the belt and its diameter. Belts are readily available at local hardware stores or home centers in grits ranging from 50-grit—a super-aggressive cut—to as high as 220-grit for finish sanding. A belt sander runs at variable speeds. The faster the motor spins, the more aggressively it will cut.

Dust collection is essential when using power sanders. What these tools do best, besides their job, is make saw dust, especially the really fine stuff that's most dangerous to your lungs. Stationary sanders are usually rigged to accept hoses for larger dust collection systems. Most belt sanders only come equipped to connect with the 2-in.-wide hoses common on most rolling shop vacuums.

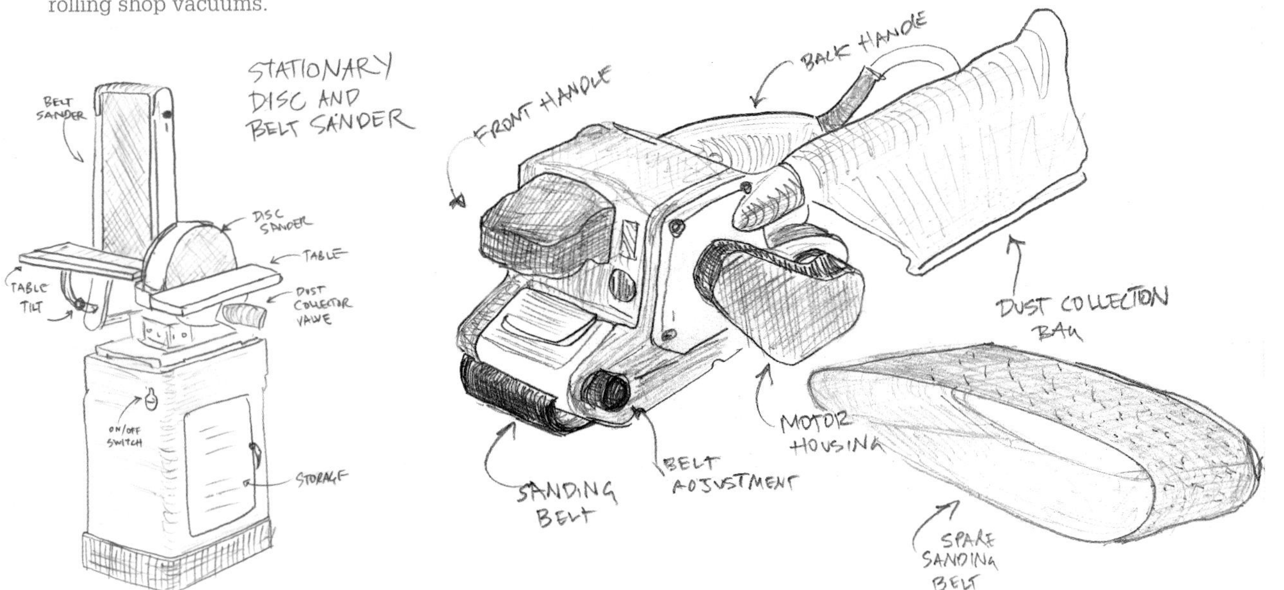

ELECTRIFY THE PROCESS
A mini Roarockit deck takes shape on the vacuum press table. The process works exactly the same as the hand-pump vacuum bag, but the air is removed with an electric pump.

UPGRADE FROM HAND-POWERED TO VACUUM-POWERED PUMP

While the Roarockit kit is a great starter tool for getting into vacuum-press veneering, there are more scalable solutions for those looking to do more demanding work or large quantities.

Many small-production skatemakers prefer an industrial-grade electric vacuum pump like those from VacuPress, a company that makes pumps for the home hobbyist and production builder.

Electric vacuum pumps work great when paired with a dedicated vacuum press table or shopmade bag. The setup I use is a table that measures about 4 ft. square. A hinged lid covered with 40 mil plastic lowers onto the table and seals around the perimeter. The vacuum pump is attached to the table from underneath with a hose. Turn the pump on, and it pulls all the air out of the bag, pressing anything inside to your form.

Another great benefit to some vacuum pumps is an automatic gauge that will restart the pump if the bag loses air and drops below a certain pressure setting.

ADD SPEED AND EASE
The VacuPress vacuum pump is an industrial-grade machine that can extract air from a vacuum bag in seconds flat. A regulator keeps a consistent pressure and turns the machine back on for a quick pump if the bag drops below that constant.

LESSONS FROM THE SKATE FACTORY

While the Roarockit method of using a one-sided mold in a vacuum press is a great solution for the small-shop skatemaker, it doesn't scale well. Try pressing 50 decks a day in vacuum bags—you'd need an army of helpers to get that right. That's why large-scale skateboard manufacturers rely exclusively on the two-part hydraulic press.

Similar to the vacuum press process, this method uses a mold to form multiple layers of veneer into a complex bend. Only instead of a single-sided mold, this process requires both sides of the mold; the veneers are pressed against the top and bottom molds using a hydraulic pump that forces the veneers to the shape of the form under thousands of pounds of pressure.

The complexity with using this technology is that the top and bottom molds are shaped to opposing complex 3D curves, and each side has a slightly different contour to account for the thickness of the deck being pressed in between. This is a complicated math calculation that I surely can't explain, and is usually solved with a computer-operated drafting and cutting system that can shape a mold exactly based on computer-rendered dimensions. But if you're looking for a work-around, there are a handful of online businesses that sell skate deck molds. They're also glad to take custom orders.

A startup skatemaker would have to make a big investment to set up shop with a traditional two-part hydraulic press and multiple molds for producing decks of different shapes and sizes—upwards of $10,000 in startup costs alone. Small-shop skatemakers have devised a number of homebrew plans to build your own two-part press for a fraction of the price (see "Make Your Own Hillbilly Press" on page 124.)

AN INDUSTRIAL SOLUTION
Acquiring a massive hydraulic skateboard press system like this is a large feat. This one came from the former World Industries, one of the original California skateboard deck manufacturers, and can press dozens of decks at once.

HYDRAULIC SHOP PRESS
For a few thousand dollars (or more depending on size and quality), a hydraulic shop press like this can be outfitted to churn out skateboard decks. Add a two-part mold made from concrete or wood and let the hydraulic motor do the hard work.

OR BUILD IT YOURSELF
Mark Edmundson's two-part press (page 124) is a shop-made version of the larger hydraulic presses found in skateboard factories.

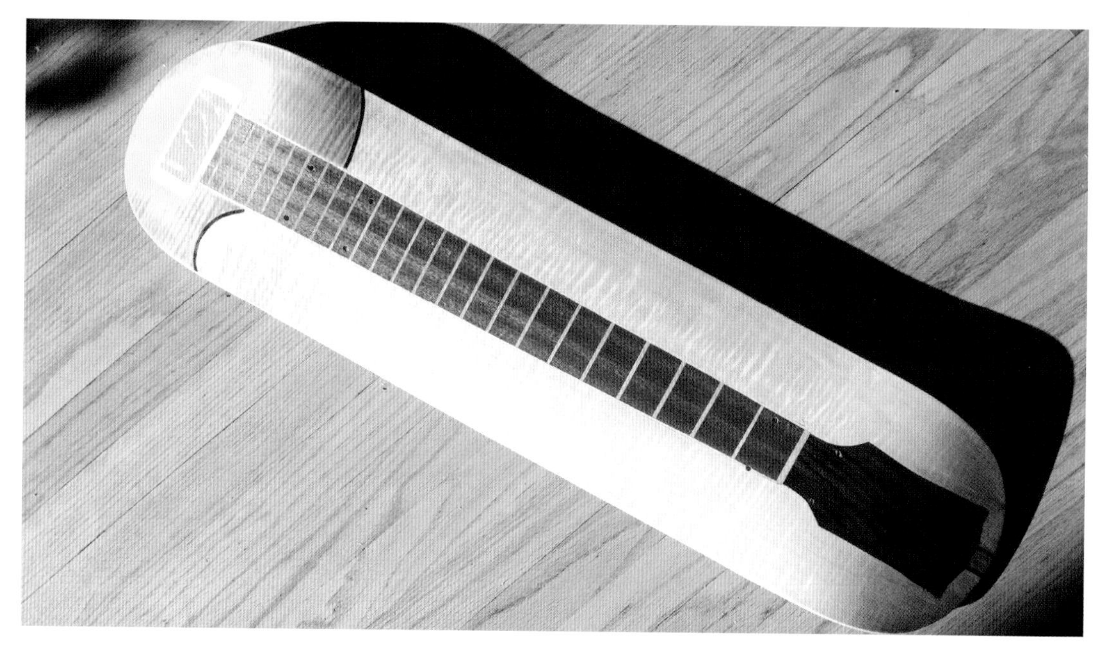

MARQUETRY CREATES CUSTOM GRAPHICS WITH WOOD

THE "GIBSON SUNBURST"
The bottom layer of this skate deck is made entirely from colorful pieces of wood assembled in a design that mimics the look of the classic Gibson sunburst guitar. Using a woodworking technique called marquetry, small pieces of thin wood are cut and assembled like a puzzle (below), and then glued to the skateboard deck (above).

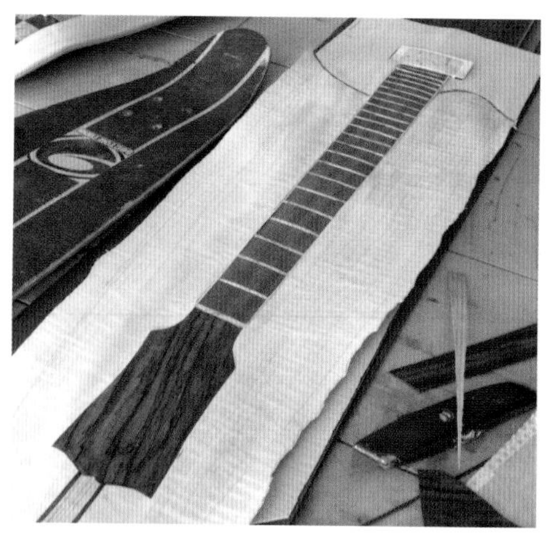

The skateboard earned its iconic cultural status thanks in part to the graphics plastered on the underside. Famous artists, graphic designers, popular brands, and everything in between have made their mark on the bottoms of skate decks with custom graphics and artwork. The blank maple skate deck offers a perfect canvas to make a statement, capture a scene, or tell a visual story. And for most skaters, the graphics serve as a personal statement.

That's why I like to create my own skateboard graphics with wood, showing off my woodworking skills using a classic technique called marquetry. The technique is hundreds of years old and first used in woodworking to decorate an object or piece of furniture with ornate pictures and designs.

Often confused with inlay—where you start with a solid piece of wood, carve away sections, then fill those voids with contrasting wood—marquetry is created using a different technique that can be easily applied to the skatemaking process. Thin sheets of wood veneer of various species are cut into small pieces and assembled like a puzzle into a design or image. The pieces are taped together with a special veneer tape and then the assembled veneer sheet is glued to a solid core—in this case your skateboard deck—using the same vacuum press process described in previous chapters. Essentially, the assembled sheet of marquetry veneer becomes the eighth layer of your skateboard deck.

To create different colors and textures in your marquetry design, use different species of wood. Designs can also be enhanced by highlighting the distinctive grain and figure in the wood.

POLKA-DOT DECK

The polka-dot design on this deck is cut and assembled using marquetry. Start by cutting out a handful of small circles, then use those as templates to cut out the corresponding shapes on your full sheet of contrasting veneer.

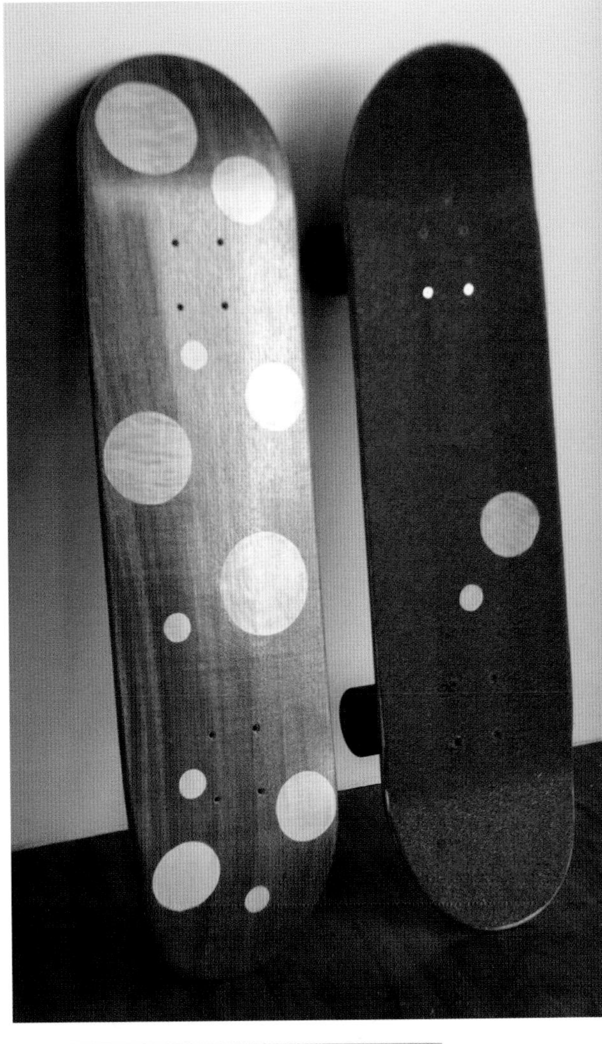

MODERN DECK DESIGN

Marquetry is not only about the shape of each piece; it's also about the wood grain. This geometric design benefits from distinct grain patterns in the wood.

MARQUETRY HOW-TO

Despite being an advanced woodworking technique, marquetry is pretty simple to try out at home because it does not require a lot of tools, equipment, or space—mostly just a lot of practice. Aside from the veneer and veneer tape, which you can order online or buy from a specialty woodworking store, the other tools and materials you'll need to get started should be readily on hand: a straight edge, a utility knife, and some wood glue.

When choosing veneers, some are better suited to beginners. Avoid veneers that are wrinkled, like burls and highly figured veneers. And avoid super-hard, brittle woods that can easily crack and split when cut with a utility knife.

Finally, try your best to buy veneer sheets that are equal in thickness so that when assembled they create a smooth, even surface.

PICK YOUR VENEERS

Decorative veneers come in a wide variety of species and wood cuts, offering different colors and textures to choose from. The most colorful woods—species like wenge (dark brown), ebony (black), bloodwood (red), and other exotic woods—are not readily available at lumber yards; you'll need to shop for them online or at a specialty woodworking store. If you need a particular color that isn't available naturally, you can start with a plain-colored wood like maple and color it with a wood dye.

DRAW YOUR DESIGN

Start by drawing out your design on paper to identify all of the pieces you will need to cut. The key is to draw the design so that it can be assembled from separate pieces of wood. Break it down into manageable components; too small, curvy, or complex and the parts will be difficult to cut out accurately. When drawing your design, consider which woods you'll use for each piece. Think about color, grain direction, and figure.

A PUZZLING DESIGN
Creating a marquetry design is a lot like making your own puzzle. Each piece must be perfectly cut to fit the pieces around it. Start by cutting the outside pieces first, then use those as templates to cut the interior pieces.

"D" IS FOR DECORATION
When creating a marquetry design, mix and match contrasting woods colors and grain patterns to make your design pop. The Maple "D" stands out when framed with wenge and a thin maple line.

1 EACH PART IS A TEMPLATE FOR THE NEXT
Tape the top template in place to cut the maple piece for the "D" (or whatever shape you choose). Before you cut it out, remove the small window of wood inside the "D," measuring from each edge to ensure that it's properly centered.

2 SCRIBE BEFORE YOU CUT
When the inside of the "D" has been removed, scribe the perimeter cut. Go slowly and stay sharp on your line. Too far inside the line and the piece will fit too loosely; go past the line and it will buckle when fit inside the frame.

3 STRAIGHT CUTS WITH A STRAIGHT EDGE
When creating a marquetry design remove the template frame once the "D" has been scribed into the veneer. Then use a straight edge to complete the cut. This will help you make straight square edges that join nicely when assembled.

4 SCRIBE THEN CUT
To cut the final piece of the "D" that fits inside the center, use the wenge off-cut so that the wood color and grain match the wenge frame. Scribe lines using the maple piece as a template.

5 MATCH THE GRAIN FOR CONTINUITY
Again, use the scribed lines as a guide to cut through the veneer with a straight edge.

CUT IT OUT

Use a sharp blade to cut the veneer, taking multiple passes until you break through the material completely. Start with a light scribe line, and then use that scribe line to guide your blade. If you're cutting a straight line, use a straight edge for the first few scribes. Once the scribe line is defined, you can cut through the material freehand.

Curved lines are much more difficult to cut, especially if the curve interferes with the natural direction of the wood grain; it's common for the blade to catch the grain and veer off from your cutline unintentionally. Cut slowly and deliberately to prevent the blade from veering off course.

Once the piece is cut, clean up any rough edges with your blade or sandpaper.

It is important that you cut your pieces to fit just right—not too tight and not too loose. The more accurate you are sizing each piece, the better your finished design will be. Too tight, and the insert piece can expand and wrinkle during the glue-up process. Too loose, and you'll be left with prominent glue lines at the seams.

MARQUETRY HOW-TO *continued*

ASSEMBLE THE DESIGN WITH VENEER TAPE

Once all of the pieces are cut to size, assemble them like a puzzle and tape them together with veneer tape. This is a special kind of tape that works just like a postage stamp: Wet down the sticky side of the tape (lick it or use a moist sponge) and press it over the seams. In a few seconds the tape will dry and hold the to pieces tightly in place.

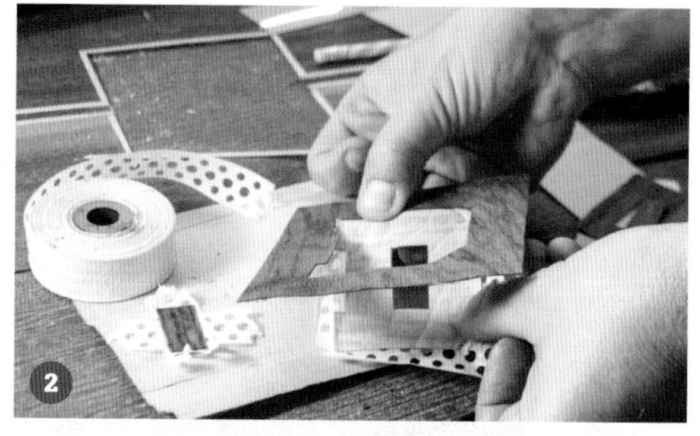

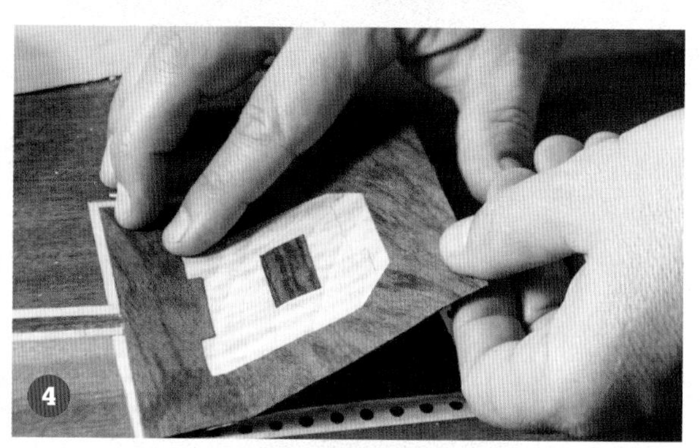

1 ASSEMBLE THE PARTS
Once all of your pieces are cut, begin assembling them into the marquetry pattern using a special veneer tape that activates with water, like a postage stamp.

2 SPECIAL PURPOSE VENEER TAPE
Veneer tape has holes so you can see through it and inspect your joining parts as you tape and during the glue up. This helps you make sure there are no gaps.

3 TAPE EVERY SEAM
Once the pieces have been taped together, flip it over to make sure all of the seams are completely taped.

4 FINAL FITTING
Once all of the parts for the "D" are assembled, drop the piece into the window and tape it in place.

5 TAPE LIBERALLY FOR A TIGHT FIT
Apply additional tape as needed to ensure that all of the pieces are tightly connected.

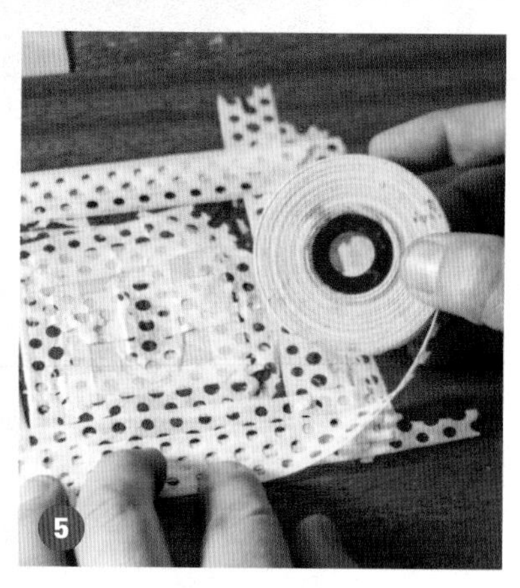

GLUE YOUR DESIGN TO A CORE

With all of the pieces taped into a single veneer sheet, now it's time to laminate it to your skateboard deck. If you built your deck in a vacuum bag, just repeat the lamination process one more time. Glue the veneer sheet in place with the taped side facing out. If you are making a flat deck, you can simply sandwich the deck and the veneer sheet between two flat boards and clamp them tightly until the glue dries.

1 THE GLUE-UP BEGINS
Start the glue-up by applying an even coat of glue across the entire surface of the skate deck. Don't leave any pools of glue or dry spots. Cut the veneer sheet to the shape of the skate deck so that when you lay it on the glue surface it doesn't hang over the edge by more than a fraction of an inch.

2 SPOT TAPE IT IN PLACE
Hold the veneer in place on the deck with a few pieces of masking tape. Then place the deck on its mold inside a vacuum bag to press it in place as the glue dries.

3 LET THE GLUE DRY
Leave the veneer in the vacuum bag under pressure for at least eight hours before you move on to the finishing process.

MARQUETRY HOW-TO *continued*

1 GIVE IT A SPONGE BATH
To remove the veneer tape, wet it down with a damp sponge and it will peel right off.

2 WET, PEEL, REPEAT
If the tape is damp enough (but not soaking wet) it should come off in long pulls and leave very little glue residue.

3 SCRAPE THE SURFACE CLEAN
A razor blade helps coax the damp veneer tape from the surface. Use it like a scraper to gently remove any residue left behind.

4 POLISH IT UP
Once all the tape is removed, sand the surface until it's perfectly flat and smooth.

5 TOO NICE TO RIDE?
No worries, this deck is a gift for Dad's retirement party and destined for the wall.

USE STENCILS TO PAINT A DESIGN

Decorating a skateboard with wood veneer marquetry is a nice touch for a longboard or cruiser deck, but it's a time-consuming process that takes some practice to get right. It also requires an investment in specialty tools and materials. With that in mind, it's not usually the wisest approach when building a standard street deck that's likely to get scuffed and thrashed. Marquetry is for boards that will get babied and cherished for a long time.

A simpler approach is to paint your deck with latex paint—either brush-on or spray-on. Paired with stencils, you can create words, intricate patterns and colorful creative designs. Also, templates can be reused. Start by drawing your design on a clear sheet of mylar, then use a sharp blade to cut away the design. Finally, tape the stencil in place and apply the paint.

Stencil-painted graphics are a poor man's alternative to the most widely used technique in the industry for adding graphics to a deck: heat transfer graphics. That industrial process works like this: Graphics are printed on super-thin sticker sheets, then positioned on the raw wood surface of a blank skate deck and carefully run through a pair of soft, heated rollers that iron the sticker onto the board. It takes a few passes through the rollers to completely bond to the wood.

Heat-transfer graphics require expensive equipment with super-hot rollers, which makes this process dangerous and out of reach for a garage or basement workshop. A handful of small-press skateboard factories around the U.S. will print batches of decks with your custom image, but they mostly require you to purchase their blank decks.

A LAYERED EFFECT

Don't limit yourself to a single stencil. Spray your deck multiple times with various colors to create a multi-layered design like this one by Michael Bozinovski at BozBoards.

THE SPRAY PAINT SOLUTION

An easy way to decorate your deck with sweet custom graphics is with spray paints and hand-cut stencils made from sheets of clear mylar.

WOOD-BURNING PEN

Woodburning, or pyrography, uses a heated metal pen similar to a soldering iron to burn a freehand design into wood. A skate deck just happens to serve as a perfect canvas for creating all sorts of charred illustrations using a combination of different pen tips, wood-burning techniques, and heat settings.

For some quick tricks of the trade, I turned to Chris Bennett, a.k.a. "Champstiles," whose elaborate pyrography illustrations are burning their way across Toronto's DIY skate scene.

"I generally like to treat it like a tattoo and burn all of my outlines first, followed by the shading in between the lines," Bennett says.

Here's how he does it: Start by laying out your design with a pencil directly onto the surface of the deck. For more complex designs, draw it in reverse on transfer paper and then transfer it to the skate deck. Next, set up your tool with the appropriate pen tips and trace and fill in the lines of your design. Finally, use the various tips and burning techniques—hatching, cross-hatching, stippling—to create shading, gradients, and depth to your design.

A basic woodburning tool kit with multiple screw-on tips for different applications won't break the bank if you are just trying it out. If you plan to stick with it, Bennett recommends upgrading your pen kit to a professional set. These heat faster, have adjustable heat settings built in, and cool down quickly, which is convenient when changing tips midway through a project.

One thing to keep in mind: Fixing woodburning mistakes is a challenge.

BURN THEN FINISH
Never burn a finished surface. Heat from your pen will react with the chemicals in the finish and create fumes that are harmful to inhale. It can also cause the surface to bubble and blur your lines.

IT'S LIKE WRITING WITH HEAT
A professional woodburning kit comes with multiple pens and tips and allows you to to adjust the heat. The adjustability comes in handy for handling different wood species that may scorch at different temperatures. For hardcore woodburners, a good tool kit will set you back between $200 and $300.

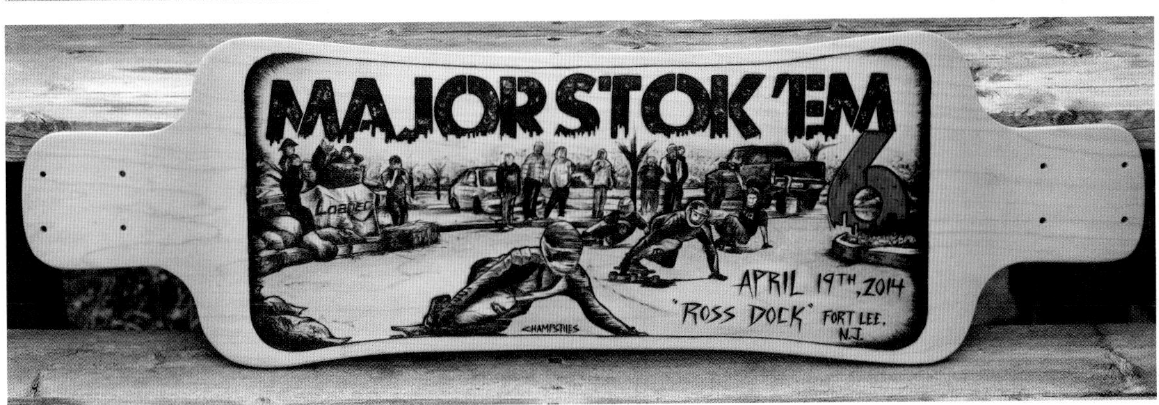

BURNED IN WOOD

These decks from Champstiles were decorated by hand using a variety of pen tips and burning techniques.

LASERS SPEED

Computer operated laser cutters make quick work of burning precise, repeatable designs in wood. Your best bet is to bring your design to a professional as a vector graphic and let them do the work.

ANCHORS AWAY

A student in one of my L.A. skateboard making woodshop hired a local laser-cutter operator to burn an anchor into the bottom of his deck. Possibilities for designs are nearly limitless.

WOOD-BURNT GRAPHICS: TWO APPROACHES

A laser engraver is an amazing tool for customizing your skate deck with a burned or cut design. These computer-operated machines are best left to the professionals, but these days you won't have trouble finding one nearby. For about thirty bucks, you can rent time and an operator to laser cut a basic design in your deck.

The one shown here is a simple anchor design downloaded from the Internet and transformed into a graphics file optimized for use with a laser engraver. With the deck placed on the cutting table, the laser is set up to cut to a certain speed and depth.

Laser cutters have a few key settings—cutting speed and depth, for instance—that can produce wildly different results from shallow etchings to deep-cut burns. A good operator will know exactly how to position the deck on the cutting table and dial-in the perfect settings for your specific design.

Laser cutters work best on flat surfaces and can't easily follow the curve of a skateboard deck, so you'll want to take that into account when you design and budget for a laser-cutting project.

BRAND YOUR BRAND

I purchased a mail-order branding iron of my SK8Makers logo. The design is CNC cut into a brass block. Heat it up with a blow torch or by placing it in an open flame (like the burners on my gas grill) for at least 15 minutes. The hotter the brand, the better the burn.

BRANDING IRON

Another method for burning a design into your deck is to use a branding iron. These days, a branding iron can be made to ordered over the Internet for a few hundred bucks, depending on the size and complexity of the design. I ordered a brand made from brass that was machine cut to match an image file of my logo.

All you have to do is send the maker an image and you get back a machine-engraved block of brass.

Using a branding iron is about as simple as it seems. Heat up the brass end of the brand until it's scalding hot—about 20 minutes on my gas grill—and then press it against your work piece for a few seconds until it burns the pattern into the wood. High-end branding irons are available with built-in heating elements. Plug in your tool to heat it up and you're ready to go. More affordable options like mine have to be heated up the old-fashioned way—with a blow torch or open fire.

SK8Makers.com

Silicon Valley, California

Visit the SK8Makers website for more shop tips, videos, workshop dates/locations, and a directory of all the tools and materials used to build the decks featured in this book. Plus, show off your skatemaking skills to the SK8Maker community. Send us photos of your handmade longboard or skateboard and help us build the world's largest gallery of one-of-a-kind decks.

Celebrate Go Skate Day

June 21st is the official holiday of skateboarding according to the International Association of Skateboard Companies. In 2013, Go Skate Day celebrated its 10-year anniversary. Learn more at

www.theiasc.org/go-skateboarding-day

Skateshops

There are thousands of independent skateboard shops around the globe where you can buy high quality trucks, wheels, bearings, grip tape and hardware. Too many to call out by name. Search for one near you with the *Thrasher Magazine* online Skateshop Locator: www.thrashermagazine.com/locate/skateshops

Skateboard Building Schools and Workshops

Stoked New York

10 Jay Street, Suite 908
Brooklyn, NY 11201
www.stoked.org
Phone: 646-710-3600

Stoked Los Angeles

10575 Virginia Ave
Culver City, CA 90232
www.stoked.org
Phone: 213-986-8272

Oasis Skateboard Factory

707 Dundas St. West
Toronto M5T 2W6
www.oasisskateboardfactory.blogspot.com/
Phone: 416-393-0845

Cal Poly ASI Craft Center

1 Grand Ave
Building 65, Room 111
San Luis Obispo, CA 93407
www.asi.calpoly.edu/wood_working
(805) 756-1266

Skateboard Veneer Sources

Roarockit Skateboard Company

880 Millwood Road
Toronto ON M4G 1X1
www.roarockit.com
1-888-857-7790

Dub Press Dist!

Rockford, Illinois 61108
www.dubpressdistribution.com
Phone: 779-770-7472

Marwood Veneer

2901 Hamburg Pike,
Jeffersonville, Indiana 47130
www.marwoodveneer.com
Phone: (812) 288-8344

Skateboard Industry Associations

International Association of Skateboard Companies
www.theiasc.org

International Skateboarding Federation
www.internationalskateboardingfederation.com

International Slalom Skateboarding Association
www.slalomskateboarder.com

International Distance Skateboard Association
www.theidsa.org

Skatepark Association International
www.spausa.org

World Freestyle Skateboard Association
www.wfsafreestyle.org

National Scholastic Skateboarding League
nsskateboardingleague.org

International Skateboard Film Festival
www.intlskateboardfilmfestival.com

Print and Online Resources

Online community of skateboard builders
www.SilverfishLongboarding.com

Skate Boarder Magazine
www.skateboardermag.com

Thrasher Magazine
www.thrashermagazine.com

Transword Skateboarding magazine
skateboarding.transworld.net

Focus Skateboard Magazine
www.focusskatemag.com

Grey Skate Magazine
www.greyskatemag.com

Sidewalk Skateboard Magazine
www.sidewalk.mpora.com

43 Magazine
www.43magazine.com

Concrete Skateboard
www.concreteskateboarding.com/

Museums and Destinations

Skateboard Hall of Fame
4226 Valley Fair Street
Simi Valley, CA 93063 USA
www.skatelab.com
Phone: (805) 578-9928

Morro Bay Skateboard Museum
699 Embarcadero
Morro Bay, California 93442
www.skatelab.com
Phone: (805) 610-3565

NHS Skateboard Museum
104 Bronson St. Suite 9
Santa Cruz, California, 95062
Phone: 831-459-7800
Skatopia Skateboard Museum
34961 Hutton Rd
Rutland, OH 45775
www.skatopia.org
Phone: 740-742-3169

index

imperial to metric conversion

Inches	mm*
1/32	0.79
3/64	1.19
1/16	1.59
5/64	1.98
3/32	2.38
7/64	2.78
1/8	3.18
9/64	3.57
5/32	3.97
11/64	4.37
3/16	4.76
13/64	5.16
7/32	5.56
15/64	5.95
1/4	6/35
17/64	6.75
9/32	7.14
19/64	7.54
5/16	7/94
21/64	8.33
11/32	8.73
23/64	9.13
3/8	9.53
25/64	9.92
13/32	10.32
27/64	10.72
7/16	11.11
29/64	11.51
31/64	11.91
1/2	12.70
33/64	13.10

Inches	mm*
17/32	13.49
35/64	13.89
9/16	14.29
37/64	14.68
19/32	15.08
39/64	15.48
5/8	15.88
41/64	16.27
21/32	16.67
43/64	17.07
11/16	17.46
45/64	17.86
23/32	18.26
47/64	18.65
3/4	19.05
49/64	19.45
25/32	19.84
51/64	20.24
13/16	20.64
53/64	21.03
27/32	21.43
55/64	21.83
7/8	22.23
57/64	22.64
29/32	23.02
59/64	23.42
15/16	23.81
61/64	24.21
31/32	24.61
63/64	25.00
1 inch	25.40

Inches	mm*
2	50.8
3	76.2
4	101.6
5	127.0
6	152.4
7	177.8
8	203.2
9	228.6
10	254.0
11	279.4
12	304.8
13	330.2
14	355.6
15	381.0
16	406.4
17	431.8
18	457.2
19	482.6
20	508.0
21	533.4
22	558.8
23	584.2
24	609.6
25	635.0
26	660.4
27	685.8
28	711.2
29	736.6
30	762.0
31	787.4
32	812.8

*Rounded to nearest 0.01 mm

About the Author

Matt Berger is a digital producer, author, and woodworker in northern California who has a passion for making things from scratch and teaching others how to do the same. Matt earned his stripes in the woodshop as an editor at *Fine Woodworking* magazine where he edited articles, and produced and starred in how-to videos featured on FineWoodworking.com. There, he honed his skills building high-quality furniture the authentic way: with hand tools, sturdy joinery, and quality hardwoods. These days, Matt practices woodworking on nights and weekends building skateboard decks out of his garage workshop, aka SK8Makers HQ, and through his series of DIY Skateboard Workshops at local schools and community centers. By day, he's a content manager for a major Silicon Valley technology company, producing video, social media, and interactive content for the web.

Acknowledgements

I couldn't have written this book without the love and support of my family, especially my wife, Mary, who puts up with all my sawdust and long hours in the shop; to my two daughters, who inspire me to build a better world; to my mom, who gave me my maker genes and helped me foster them from an early age; and my dad, for teaching me to be responsible and to strive for success.

To the entire crew at SkateLab and the Skateboard Hall of Fame in Simi Valley, California, for schooling me on all things skateboard. Especially Todd Huber and his amazing collection of historic skateboard decks, and Steve Badillo, who was kind enough to teach a Barney like me how to set up a deck like a pro.

To the ASI Craft Center at Cal Poly State University in San Luis Obispo where I built my first skateboard 20 years ago and learned that there is nothing I can't build if I set my mind to it. To the entire crew at *Fine Woodworking* magazine for opening me up to the amazing world of woodworking. And to Bob and Scott at Community Woodshop L.A. for sharing your space to help spread the skatemaker bug.

To all those who contribute to the growing handmade skateboard community. In particular, Ted and Norah Hunter at Roarockit Skateboard for all that you have done to contribute to this book, for innovating the tools and materials that democratized the business. And to the Silverfish Longboarding community for creating a place for skatemakers like me to share, learn and inspire.

And to my editor, Matthew Teague, and publisher, Paul McGahren, for giving me this opportunity to help teach the world to make things from scratch, by hand, one skateboard at a time.